Compliments

of

Sunnen Products Company

James K Bertholf

**CHAIRMAN OF THE BOARD
AND PRESIDENT**

ST. LOUIS

GATEWAY TO TOMORROW

A Contemporary Portrait by Betty Burnett

"St. Louis' Enterprises"
by Martha Baker

Windsor Publications, Inc.
Chatsworth, California

ST. LOUIS
GATEWAY TO TOMORROW

A Contemporary Portrait by Betty Burnett

Windsor Publications, Inc.—Book Division
Managing Editor: Karen Story
Design Director: Alexander D'Anca
Photo Director: Susan L. Wells
Executive Editor: Pamela Schroeder

Staff for *St. Louis: Gateway to Tomorrow*
Manuscript Editor: Douglas P. Lathrop
Photo Editor: Larry Molmud
Editor, Corporate Profiles: Melissa Wells
Production Editor, Corporate Profiles: Justin Scupine
Proofreader: Mary Jo Scharf
Customer Service Manager: Phyllis Feldman-Schroeder
Editorial Assistants: Dominique Jones, Kim Kievman,
    Michael Nugwynne, Kathy B. Peyser, Theresa J. Solis
Publisher's Representatives, Corporate Profiles: Ken
    Fiebig, Joe Mihm
Art Director: Ellen Ifrah
Layout Artist, Corporate Profiles: Lisa Barrett
Layout Artist, Editorial: Michael Burg

Windsor Publications, Inc.
Elliot Martin, Chairman of the Board
James L. Fish III, Chief Operating Officer
Michele Sylvestro, Vice President/Sales-Marketing
Mac Buhler, Vice President/Acquisitions

Library of Congress Cataloging-in-Publication Data
Burnett, Betty, 1940-
St. Louis : gateway to tomorrow : a contemporary portrait /
    by Betty Burnett. — 1st ed.
    p. cm.
    Includes bibliographical references and index.
ISBN: 0-89781-342-1 : $32.95
    1. Saint Louis (Mo.)—Civilization. 2. Saint Louis (Mo.)—
Description—Views. 3. Saint Louis (Mo.)—Economic
conditions. 4. Saint Louis (Mo.)—Industries. I. Title.
II. Title: Saint Louis.
F474.S25B87   1990   90-44197
972'.66—dc20   CIP

FRONTISPIECE:

Photo courtesy HMS

Group, Inc.

RIGHT: Photo by

Gary Bohn

Contents

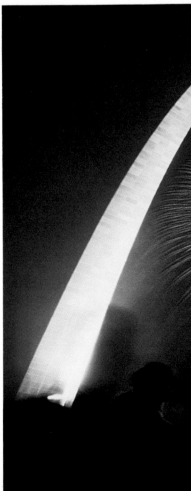

PART ONE

Gateway To Tomorrow

The main entertainment
area at the Jefferson
National Expansion Me-
morial (Gateway Arch
grounds) during the
Veiled Prophet Fair is
a sea of people. Photo
by Wes Paz

CHAPTER ONE

Breaking Ground

"Chouteau, you will come here as soon as navigation opens, and will cause this place to be cleared, in order to form our settlement after the plan that I shall give you."

—*Pierre Laclède Ligueste to Auguste Chouteau, 1763*

In the 1840s, some 80 years after its founding by Pierre Laclède, St. Louis earned the title "Gateway to the West." It was then a bustling river city, teeming with Easterners itching to go West, with young entrepreneurs seeking their fortunes, and with newly immigrated German and Irish families.

Today St. Louis is a gateway to a new frontier, a frontier of high technology, biomedical engineering, telecommunications, and information processing. Its financial and commercial networks reach across the world, just as its trade routes once stretched across the American wilderness.

But even before St. Louis was the Gateway City, it was the Mound City. The Hopewell people, who lived in the area between 500 B.C. and 400 A.D., were known as "mound builders" for the earthen mounds they constructed.

The Charleston had them dancing in the streets of St. Louis throughout the "Roaring Twenties." Courtesy, Missouri Historical Society

The agrarian Hopewells were traders who exchanged goods with tribes throughout the country. They probably also studied astronomy, as their mounds fit the compass points. Many mounds remain as relics of that great civilization across the Mississippi River in Illinois' Cahokia Mounds State Park.

Thirteen hundred years after the Hopewells left the area, French trader Pierre Laclède Ligueste and his protege, 14-year-old Auguste Chouteau, traveled upriver from New Orleans looking for a site for a trading post. In December 1763 Laclède found the perfect place—a plateau on a rocky bluff near the confluence of the Missouri and Mississippi rivers.

Laclède named his new village St. Louis in honor of the patron saint of the reigning French king, Louis XV. In the early spring of 1764 a party headed by Chouteau began to clear away the timber and started construction. Ironically, soon after the village's founding, the villagers learned that all the French territory on the west side of the river had been ceded to Spain.

At the same time, the area on the east side of the Mississippi River (now Illinois) also lost its French nationality and became English. Many French Catholics did not want to become English subjects and moved to St. Louis. Although Spain ruled the area for 35 years, the town was allowed to remain French in custom, atti-

tude, and language until after the U.S. government bought the vast area known as Louisiana in 1803.

As soon as President Thomas Jefferson concluded the Louisiana Purchase, he dispatched two explorers, Meriwether Lewis and William Clark, to survey the territory, which reached to the Continental Divide. Two years and four months after they left Missouri—during which time they traveled through 7,000 miles of wilderness, going all the way to the Pacific Ocean—Lewis and Clark returned to the village of St. Louis. When their boats docked, most of the town was there to greet them, cheering their courage.

At the time of the explorers' departure, St. Louis was an American city. Napoleon had won the Louisiana Territory from Spain in 1800, yet the Spanish continued to govern the city of St. Louis. The transfer of land to the United States in 1804 proceeded in two steps. The Spanish flag came down on March 9, 1804, and, according to tradition, the French Tricolor was flown for 24 hours to acknowledge its French heritage. Then the Stars and Stripes was raised.

At that time St. Louis had a population of about 1,000 people, mostly French Catholic. By 1820 the number was over 4,000, with most English-speaking and Protestant.

The lure of the fur trade brought hundreds of hope-

In 1817 the first steamboat, the tiny *Zebulon Pike*, docked in St. Louis. Within 10 years steamboat traffic on the Mississippi and Missouri rivers was heavy, and at least one steamboat docked each day of good weather. After another 10 years, in 1837, the city was second only to New Orleans in tonnage of river traffic.

One of St. Louis' most important residents, the English-born Henry Shaw, arrived by steamboat in 1819. Shaw quickly built a lucrative hardware business and an elegant estate, which he later gave to the city as Tower Grove Park. While still a young man, Shaw had a dream of creating a world-famous botanical garden which would provide useful information to botanists and gardeners alike. His dream was realized in the Missouri Botanical Garden, which he also donated to the city.

The steamboats also brought the dreaded cholera to the city. Throughout the 1830s and 1840s river cities such as New Orleans, Cincinnati, and St. Louis suffered greatly from periodic epidemics. An estimated one-tenth of the city's population of 70,000 was struck down by the disease in 1849.

Five years later, in the midst of the worst cholera epidemic, fire broke out on the *White Cloud*, a steamboat moored at a city dock. As was the custom, the boat was cut loose with the hope that it would burn itself out. A freak wind pushed it into boat after boat as it drifted downstream. Twenty-three boats caught fire, and the wind carried sparks to the cargo stacked up on Wharf Street. From there the fire spread to the city. Building after building blazed. Gunpowder was used to create a firebreak and eventually the fire died down. The property loss was put at $6.1 million, including 400 buildings and 15 city blocks.

Although the first American railroad had been built in 1826, it was not until 1851 that the railroad came to St. Louis, primarily because the river seemed an insurmountable barrier. In 1865 service between St. Louis and Kansas City was initiated, and access to the West was opened.

Access to the East, however, had to wait another 10 years, until the Eads Bridge spanned the Mississippi. The bridge was officially opened for carriage traffic on July 4, 1874, in a jubilant daylong celebration. The age

il entrepreneurs to St. Louis. Outfitters for the western ade joined fur traders in turning a profit. Hawken rifles and Murphy wagons were produced in St. Louis, as vell as ropes, chains, wagon wheels, and hundreds of ardware items.

The Santa Fe trade was of vital importance to St. ouis. Large quantities of Mexican silver—averaging omething over $100,000 per year—came to Missouri ia the Santa Fe traders. Much of it found its way to St. ouis, giving the city a substantial hard money supply nd stimulating economic growth.

Protecting the nation's interest in the West was the uty of the U.S. Cavalry. In 1826 Jefferson Barracks was reated south of St. Louis as a military camp. For its rst 20 years the barracks served as a frontier outpost r soldiers fighting the Indian Wars. The noted Sac hief Black Hawk was held a prisoner there.

of the cumbersome ferry was over, and as other railroad bridges were constructed, the transport of goods by rail became an integral part of the St. Louis economy. Today the St. Louis region is the nation's second largest rail center.

In the 1850s a controversial court case put St. Louis in the news across the nation. Dred Scott, a black slave, sued for his freedom in 1846 because he had been held as a slave in free territory. Scott and his St. Louis attorneys claimed that once he left slave territory he and his wife, Harriet, should have been freed. A lower court agreed, but his owner appealed and eventually the case reached the Supreme Court. Since Scott had returned to St. Louis, where slavery was legal, Southern sympathizers claimed that he accepted slavery.

The Supreme Court heard arguments on the case for several weeks, while newspapers across the nation

FACING PAGE, TOP: The splendor and opulence of late-nineteenth-century St. Louis is captured in this lithograph from Hart's Capital Oyster Saloon. Courtesy, Missouri Historical Society

BELOW: Still one of St. Louis' key landmarks, the Eads Bridge is shown under construction in December 1873. Courtesy, Missouri Historical Society

FACING PAGE, BOTTOM: The post-Civil War years saw many industrial concerns thrive in St. Louis. Courtesy, Missouri Historical Society

took sides. Finally, Chief Justice Roger B. Taney ruled in 1857 that slaves were not citizens and therefore the provisions of the Fifth Amendment (the "due process" clause) did not apply to them. Abolitionists were incensed and the nation became more divided.

On the eve of the Civil War, St. Louis was a divided city. Its many Southern-born residents were Confederate sympathizers and some continued to hold slaves, although there were relatively few slaves in the city. Freeborn blacks and freed slaves found limited opportunity in the area as steamboat stewards or barbers. A few became well-to-do through real estate transactions. Wanting to improve opportunities for his race, the Reverend James Berry Meacham defied state law by teaching black children to read and write in a "floating school" in the middle of the Mississippi River.

In 1861 the Missouri governor, Claiborne Jackson, was pro-Confederacy, while St. Louis Congressman Frank Blair (later a major general with Sherman) was strongly pro-Union. The showdown between their supporters came on May 10, 1861, less than a month after Fort Sumter had surrendered to Confederates.

Nine hundred members of the Southern Guard bivouacked at Lindell Grove, near Grand and Lindell boulevards, which they named Camp Jackson in honor of the governor. Led by Captain Nathaniel Lyon, Union forces (including recruits from the city's German neighborhoods) attacked the encampment.

As many as 6,000 men moved in on the rebels. Thousands of spectators gathered to watch the confrontation. The roundup of Confederate sympathizers was easily completed, but as the Union soldiers waited for orders to move their prisoners to the arsenal, many local Southern sympathizers—some of them well-known citizens—cursed the Union troops and threw rocks at them.

The Union soldiers reacted in kind and the fighting grew more heated. Someone fired shots and suddenly soldiers, volunteers, and civilians were involved in a bloody riot. Before it ended, some 25 persons lay dead and many more had been wounded. Bitterness over the battle—the only one in the city—lasted for many years.

In the years following the Civil War, St. Louis boomed, becoming the nation's "fourth city" and the third greatest manufacturing city. Iron production, milling, brewing, cloth manufacturing, and the furniture industry employed thousands of workers. Limestone quarries and brickyards supplied material for the burgeoning construction industry.

Dozens of small breweries dotted the neighborhoods of St. Louis in the years before the Civil War. In 1876 a brewer named Adolphus Busch developed a beer that he called Budweiser. In an aggressive marketing campaign, Busch dubbed Budweiser "the king of beers," and before long the nation was agreeing with him.

A dark cloud briefly dimmed the city's optimism. One of the several scandals that dogged the administration of President U.S. Grant involved the whiskey producers of St. Louis. The city was then a major distilling center. A scheme to circumvent federal regulations was concocted and federal agents were bribed to affix bogus seals to the bottles indicating that federal liquor taxes had been paid. Distillers, middlemen, and top officials were all caught in a "Whiskey Ring," which was de-

frauding the government of hundreds of thousands of dollars each year.

Grant's ties to St. Louis were strong. His wife, Julia Dent, grew up in the area, and the family lived in a log cabin which later was moved to Grant's Farm, now owned by Anheuser-Busch and open to the public.

In the late nineteenth century a group of civic-minded businessmen came up with an idea to commemorate the centennial of the Louisiana Purchase—a world's fair. The 1904 St. Louis World's Fair (technically the Louisiana Purchase Exposition) was one of the greatest events in the city's history, and in the nation's. The spirit of excitement that the fair stirred was captured in the 1944 movie *Meet Me in St. Louis,* and inspired a popular song. Millions of Americans today still recognize the bouncy chorus: "Meet me in St. Louie, Louie/Meet me at the fair. . ."

President Theodore Roosevelt opened the fair from the White House on April 30, 1904, by flicking a switch that set the lights at Forest Park ablaze. At that moment 10,000 flags rose from domes, towers, and flagstaffs. John Philip Sousa raised his baton, the trumpets rang out, and 400 voices sang "Hymn of the West."

Forty-four nations participated in the fair, an unheard-of number, and 14 palaces were constructed, providing 5 million square feet of exhibit space. The outdoor exhibits filled another 6 million square feet. The first Olympic games to be held in the United States opened to a cheering crowd. An automobile race, several short dirigible flights, and telegraphy exhibits demonstrated the wonders of modern technology.

During the seven months that the fair was open, almost 20 million visitors oohed and ahhed over the spectacle. A sense of pride enveloped St. Louis, and a "City Beautiful" campaign kept streets clean and yards attractive. This cooperation is seen today in the Veiled Prophet Fair, which draws visitors from across the nation and the world each July.

In 1927 Charles Lindbergh brought new attention to the city when he landed *The Spirit of St. Louis* in Paris. Lindbergh had worked as an airmail pilot for the St. Louis-based Robertson Aircraft Company and found enthusiastic backers in the city for his proposed New York-to-Paris flight.

The city role in the development of aviation has been dramatic. Civic leaders such as Albert Bond Lambert (who developed the city's airport) generously supported the fledgling industry in the 1920s. Oliver Parks gambled on its success and opened Parks Air College in 1927 to train flight technicians. Robertson Aircraft Corporation and Curtiss-Wright Airplane Manufacturing

Company had large installations near the airport. Today McDonnell Douglas Corporation, which began modestly in 1939 in a second-story rented office, employs 120,000 people worldwide and brings in over $13 billion in sales. Dozens of manufacturing firms ancillary to the aerospace industry are located in St. Louis, as is TWA's domestic hub. Lambert Field has become the eighth busiest airport in the nation.

While both the aerospace and automotive industries in St. Louis are vital to the city's prosperity, its economy is diversified and dispersed, which means that recessions—even the Great Depression of the 1930s—have not hurt the city as badly as some cities.

The strength of that diversity was seen during World War II, when 75 percent of its manufacturing concerns converted to defense production. The best-known defense installation was U.S. Cartridge (or St. Louis Ordnance), which produced billions of rounds of ammunition and, with 35,000 employees, was the largest plant of its kind in the world.

During the war 150,000 young men and women left St. Louis to join the armed services, and 98 percent of them returned. Many of them came home because of the efforts of two St. Louis manufacturers, Monsanto Chemical Company and Nooter Boiler Company. Monsanto produced fungicides, sulfa, and other drugs; Nooter built the tank that allowed for the commercial production of penicillin.

Postwar St. Louis, like all major cities across the nation, experienced a great building boom. Established suburbs expanded and new suburbs were created, as young families, with the help of VA loans, found they could afford homes. Because most of the residential development was in the county, the inner city began to deteriorate. During the 1960s several manufacturing concerns moved out of the city, following residents into the suburbs. Some left the area altogether for the Sun Belt.

Two new construction projects—Busch Stadium and the Gateway Arch—kept the city alive. The Jefferson National Memorial (the Arch) had been planned for almost 30 years when the first concrete was poured in 1962. By the time it was topped out in 1965, it had already become a symbol for the city and for the great surge of pioneers who "won the West" in the nineteenth century.

Busch Stadium, home of the St. Louis Cardinals baseball team, also opened in 1965. Throughout their history, the Cardinals frequently have finished the season near the top of the National League. During the 1980s the team won the pennant three times and the

An authentic Ferris Wheel of spectacular proportions dominated the sky over the 1904 World's Fair in St. Louis. Courtesy, Missouri Historical Society

ABOVE AND FAC-
ING PAGE: Union
Station was a busy
transportation hub
even at the beginning
of the new century.
Courtesy, Missouri
Historical Society

World Series once.

Despite the completion of the Arch and its Museum of Westward Expansion and the subsequent increase in tourism, the early 1970s were probably the low point for St. Louis. The city's diminishing resources seemed to present an insurmountable obstacle to economic health.

But the determination of a few key businessmen initiated a turnaround that continues to this day. Civic Progress, an organization of area chief executive officers, used its influence to get important bond issues passed. Donald E. Lasater committed his Mercantile Bank to scores of redevelopment projects that gave a new spirit of optimism to the city. Leon Strauss, head of Pantheon Corporation, also made the assumption that the city would revive and began extensive rehabilitation of existing buildings. Sverdrup Corporation, Centerre Bank, and Southwestern Bell expanded their downtown facilities. The mammoth Cervantes Convention and Exhibit Center (which is slated for expansion) opened downtown in 1977.

As the city began to prepare for new growth, labor and management made a concerted effort to work together harmoniously and formed PRIDE, an association that stresses cooperation in the building trades. St. Louis has always been a strong union town; today it is considered a *good* labor town, with a highly skilled, well-paid, cooperative labor force. "On time and at cost" are familiar words to St. Louis builders and developers.

The 1980s has seen a great surge of growth for the area. Since 1980, 170,000 new jobs have been added and $18 billion in construction has been completed. The city leads the nation in historic preservation and renovation. The rebirth of Union Station as a tourist attraction and the completion of St. Louis Centre, the nation's largest and most successful downtown indoor shopping center, have revitalized retail trade downtown.

The educational institutions in St. Louis, especially Washington University, St. Louis University, and Webster University, draw students from across the nation. Fifty-six hospitals and two medical schools have made

the area into a leading medical center.

Today St. Louis is more of a region than a city. Its immediate trade area encompasses 10 counties, five in Missouri and five in Illinois. The metropolitan population is almost 2,500,000 and the effective buying income is $35,000 per household. Housing costs have been called "the most affordable in the U.S." for several years, despite the fact that the great majority of St. Louis homes are made of brick.

St. Louis is at the hub of the nation's transportation network. It functions as the midcontinent switchyards for the 7,000-mile inland waterways system. Twenty-five barge lines serve the region and public docks dot the city's 19 miles of shoreline. Four interstate highways keep traffic moving smoothly through the area.

Fifteen major corporations call St. Louis home, and at last count 320 *Fortune* 500 companies operated major offices or facilities in the region. These companies have contributed greatly to the cultural and social life of the city, making its quality of life one of the highest in the nation.

St. Louis city and county governments have been separate entities since 1876. At times the rivalry between the two has been intense. Today that rivalry is symbolized by the annual boat race on the Mississippi between the mayor and the county executive.

But cooperation between the two governments is more common than competition. The new Cultural District, the City-County Hospital, and the Regional Arts Commission, as well as the Regional Commerce and Growth Association, indicate a new emphasis on regional planning.

In 1980 St. Louis received bad press across the nation when census figures showed a sharp drop in population within the city limits. The city was written off as hopelessly decayed and decrepit. Today it is characterized as "the decade's leading comeback city." The renaissance has created an air of excitement that can be matched by few cities. But the renaissance did not happen spontaneously. It came about because of the dedication and hard work of a handful of leaders—and through the courage of a city that believed in itself.

CHAPTER TWO

Solid Foundations

"St. Louis considered itself the only civilized city on the Mississippi, after New Orleans, of course. Every boulevard bespoke grandeur and Europe . . . The Civil War accounted for most of the monuments . . . and the buildings were graced in marble and granite . . ."

—Ntozake Shange
Betsy Brown

Today St. Louis prides itself on being a city of distinguished neighborhoods. When asked where they live, St. Louisans are likely to respond, "Shaw," "Soulard," "U City," "Webster," or "the Hill," rather than give a street address. The newcomer to St. Louis quickly learns which neighborhoods are which and what each has to offer.

The heart of the St. Louis region is downtown, the area extending west from the river to Jefferson Avenue, north to Dr. Martin Luther King Boulevard, and south to Chouteau Avenue. St. Louis, like Chicago and Washington, D.C., is well known for its extraordinary architecture, architecture that is well worth studying and admiring. There is a blend of the old and

Although a tree climber may seem to be near its apex, the Gateway Arch actually towers 630 feet high— 75 feet taller than the Washington Monument. Photo by Gary Bohn

20

The Old Cathedral is the oldest cathedral west of the Mississippi. The land was the site of a log church before America was a nation. Photo by G. Robert Bishop/ HMS Group, Inc.

the new, of stone and glass, of green space and concrete.

Dominating the St. Louis skyline is the Gateway Arch, one of the most-visited tourist attractions in the nation and certainly the number-one attraction in the city. It is the nation's most dramatic monument—630 feet high—and is as wide as it is tall—630 feet in span.

Designed by the great Finnish architect Eero Saarinen in 1948, the Arch was not completed until 1965. Before construction could begin, some 40 blocks of warehouses had to be cleared and a half-mile of railroad relocated. The Arch was engineered to deflect only 18 inches in a 150-mph wind. Inside, cable-operated transporters carry visitors up each leg to an observation deck. (The most-asked question about the top of the Arch is "Where's the restaurant?" There isn't one.)

The magnificent Museum of Westward Expansion beneath the Arch depicts the history of the development of the American West. Operated by the National Park Service as part of the Jefferson National Expansion Memorial, the museum is designed in concentric arcs instead of in formal, linear hallways, giving the visitor the pleasantly eerie feeling of floating through time.

Framed by the Arch is the Old Courthouse, also maintained by the National Park Service. Begun in 1839, the building is topped by a Renaissance dome predating the dome of the U.S. Capitol. In the years before the Civil War, the Old Courthouse was the scene of occasional slave auctions and of the historic Dred Scott decision.

Near the base of the Arch is the neoclassical Old Cathedral, more properly called the Basilica of St. Louis, King of France. The site was reserved for a church in 1764, when the town was founded, and has served as a place of worship continuously for 225 years. The pre-

sent building was erected in 1834 and was extensively and elegantly renovated in 1963.

Eads Bridge distinguishes the riverfront. It was the world's first steel-truss bridge and had the longest arches built up to its time. Eads was the first bridge to cross the Mississippi at St. Louis. For its opening on July 4, 1874, the city celebrated all day and all night with parades, speeches, and fireworks.

Today the Poplar Street Bridge, carrying I-55, I-70, and I-64 across the Mississippi, is more widely used than the Eads, McKinley, or Martin Luther King bridges. The Poplar Street Bridge was formally christened the Bernard F. Dickmann Memorial Bridge for the mayor who first promoted development of the riverfront.

In the shadow of Eads Bridge is Laclede's Landing. Formerly a warehouse district, the historic nine-block area of cobblestone streets has been restored building by building while maintaining the original Creole block plan. Restaurants, bars, and shops line the area, which slopes to the levee. It is one of the most popular nightlife centers in St. Louis, treating clubgoers to all types of music—jazz, blues, soft and hard rock, punk, and experimental.

Several mock riverboats are docked along the riverfront. Two house fast-food restaurants and two are excursion boats. The famous *Goldenrod*, the showboat that inspired Edna Ferber's novel, *Showboat* (and the subsequent musical), recently moved to St. Charles and still offers dinner theater entertainment. The drive along the riverfront, originally renamed Wharf Street, was recently renamed Leonor K. Sullivan Boulevard in honor of the late congresswoman noted for her work

on inland waterways transportation.

For the past 15 years downtown St. Louis has experienced an exciting renaissance, which has accelerated within the last five years. Downtown is the cornerstone of the regional economy and the largest employment center in the area, with well over 110,000 people working there. Metro Link, a light rail line, will make a major contribution to the vitality of downtown when it opens in 1993. Office buildings, retail establishments, and residential property—both modest and luxurious—are well integrated. Downtown is also successfully integrated, racially and ethnically.

Like other major cities, however, St. Louis has a problem with the homeless. About 10,000 men, women, and children in the area find themselves without a place to live over the course of a year, and many of them congregate downtown. Several resources are available to them. The city recently opened Hope House, a temporary residence for families managed by the American Red Cross, and churches and other charitable organizations sponsor 21 other shelters.

Best-known among the city's champions of the homeless is the Reverend Larry Rice, whose New Life Evangelistic Center downtown provides shelter for

The back of the old Western Union building offers a unique vantage point for a parade-watcher. Photo by Odell Mitchell

thousands of people each year. Other successful community-inspired programs that assist the poor include the "Dollar Help" project of Laclede Gas Company and the "Dollar More" project of Union Electric. Customers may pay an extra dollar each month to offset the utility bill of someone who cannot pay.

Several corporate headquarters and major business institutions are located downtown. Two leading banks, Boatmen's and Mercantile, built towers to emphasize their commitment to the city.

The Edison Brothers headquarters was designed by the St. Louis-based firm of Hellmuth, Obata, and Kassabaum, which also designed the MCI Building and the 44-story One Bell Center, new headquarters for Southwestern Bell.

One of St. Louis' most famous buildings is the

St. Louis' historic role as "Gateway to the West" is immortalized in the famed Gateway Arch. Completed in 1965, the monument speaks of vision, drive, and optimism— and above all, it says "St. Louis." Photo by John Elk III

Wainwright, designed by architect Louis Sullivan and constructed in 1891 as the world's first skyscraper. It has been called "the most significant building of modern architecture's early years" because Sullivan used a steel frame instead of concrete or masonry. It is now a state office building.

St. Louis Centre, with 1.5 million square feet, is the largest enclosed downtown mall in the United States. Barringer Fifield, in *Seeing St. Louis,* describes St. Louis Centre as "reminiscent, in all its glassy glory, of Milan's nineteenth-century *galleria.*" The center contains 150 shops and restaurants and connects the two downtown department stores, Famous-Barr and Dillard's. Centered over the mall is a 20-story office building.

The most exciting shopping area downtown is found in the restored Union Station at 18th and Market streets. The 42-acre Romanesque Revival station fell into decay as passenger rail travel declined. For years it stood vacant and was threatened with destruction. Its conversion into a commercial complex, housing restaurants, boutiques, ballrooms, and a hotel, was completed in 1985 at a cost of $140 million. Today it is one of the most popular entertainment spots in town, and a 10-screen movie theater has recently been added.

Green space hopscotches across downtown, from the expanse of the Arch grounds to the Aloe Plaza across from Union Station. The newest park area is the three-block Gateway Mall, which abuts the controversial Richard Serra sculpture, *Twain.* The eight rusting steel plates making up the sculpture were arranged to give the viewer a sense of the earth, rather than a sense of upliftment, as more traditional monuments do.

Traditional sculpture can be found in the Milles Fountain at Aloe Plaza, a powerful depiction of mermaids and mermen, naiads and tritons. Titled *The Meeting of the Waters,* the sculpture symbolizes the junction of the Mississippi and Missouri rivers.

More tradition is found along Market Street, which divides the city into north and south. It could also be called "Government Row." In the seven blocks between 18th and 11th streets are the main post office, two federal buildings, the municipal courts, the city hall (modeled after the Paris Hotel de Ville), the federal courts, and the civil courts. Kiel Auditorium, just west of the city hall, serves as an exhibition center and concert auditorium.

On the north flank of downtown is the Cervantes Convention Center, now slated for dramatic expansion as convention business continues to grow. Since 1983

the number meetings and conventions hosted in St. Louis each year has risen 116 percent, mainly because of the city's affordable accommodations and easy accessibility. Such diverse groups as the Southern Baptist Convention, Lions International, and the Popular Culture Association have chosen St. Louis for their national conventions.

Thousands of hotel rooms are available downtown, most within walking distance of attractions, and several new luxury hotels are planned for the area to complement the growing convention and tourism business.

On the southern flank of downtown is Busch Memorial Stadium, de-

signed jointly by Sverdrup Corporation, a well-known St. Louis-based engineering firm, and Edward Stone. The home of the baseball Cardinals, it has seen five World Series contests and an All-Star game. The playing field in the 50,000-seat stadium is below street level, giving Busch a fairly low profile.

Residential areas downtown include the luxurious Mansion House Center (which overlooks the river), Plaza Square apartments near Union Station, and Columbus Square, just north of the Convention Center. New homes developed by Mark Conner in the same area offer elegant suburban living in the city, with spacious rooms, yards, attached garages, and all modern amenities.

According to national sources, St. Louis offers one of the "most affordable" major housing markets in the nation—about 28 percent below the national average. A remarkable housing rehabilitation program in the city neighborhoods has resulted in St. Louis' being hailed by the National Housing Rehabilitation Associ-

ation as "the city doing the most to rebuild and repair housing stock."

While the most distinctive characteristic of St. Louis housing is its brickwork, many building styles are available. Numerous executive-level suburban communities offer prime living areas within a 20- to 30-minute drive of downtown.

Home buyers in St. Louis generally need less income to qualify for their purchases and have lower monthly mortgage payments than their counterparts in other metropolitan areas. Studies indicate that average mortgage payments among St. Louisans represent 20 percent of their income. The average cost of living in St. Louis is about 3 percent lower than the average for all metropolitan areas nationwide, according to the American Chamber of Commerce Researchers Association (ACCRA). Property taxes are also significantly below national averages.

Beyond Martin Luther King Drive is the near North Side, an area with more than its share of derelict buildings and other problems associated with poverty. Several public housing projects, most notably Cochran Gardens, have been successful in that area because of tenant involvement under the leadership of black activist Bertha Gilkey. Housing in the nearby Jeff-Vander-Lou area is for moderate income families.

Immediately south of downtown is the Soulard district, oldest residential area in the city and rich in history. Named for a refugee from the French Revolution, Soulard was also referred to as "Frenchtown" in its early days because of its distinct French influence. During the nineteenth century Germans, Hungarians, Croatians, Italians, Serbs, Bohemians, and Lebanese also settled in Soulard. Today the neighborhood is undergoing a tremendous revitalization spearheaded by the Soulard Restoration Group, an association of homeowners and other interested people who want to maintain the neighborhood's charm while introducing modern comforts. New construction fits in with and is scarcely detectable from the old.

At the northern edge of the district is the Soulard Market, a public produce market that has been in operation for two centuries. The present Italian Renaissance-style building was erected by the city in 1929.

Some of the city's largest industrial plants are located in Soulard—Monsanto's Queeny plant, Nooter Corporation, Welsh Baby Carriage Company, and "the brewery." Today "the brewery" refers only to Anheuser-Busch, although at one time as many as a dozen breweries thrived in St. Louis. A longtime landmark, Anheuser-Busch is one of the area's largest employers and contributes greatly to the city's cultural life.

Lafayette Square, just northwest of Soulard, was the first neighborhood in St. Louis to be designated as a historic district and placed on the National Register.

Ralston Purina invested heavily in bringing the nearby LaSalle neighborhood back to life. Several blocks of turn-of-the-century townhouses were restored by the company. Pet, Inc. (now a part of Whitman Co.), also invested in the neighborhood.

South St. Louis, stretching from Arsenal Street to the county line, has a personality all its own, as chronicled by *Post-Dispatch* columnist Elaine Viets. "Its faults are the same as its virtues: The people are hardworking, hardheaded and independent," she writes in *Urban Affairs*. "That's what you say when you like them. Otherwise, they're stodgy, stubborn workaholics." Neat one- and two-family red brick homes centered in small, well-tended lawns characterize the South Side. The area celebrates its German heritage each fall during Bevo Days.

The Hill, also on the South Side, is known for its Italian atmosphere, even though it was originally home to English settlers. Sculptor Rudy Torrini's moving tribute to Italian immigrants is located in front of St. Ambrose Church. Many Italian restaurants and bakeries dot the area. Italian festivals are held frequently.

Nearby is the Shaw neighborhood, named for its proximity to the Missouri Botanical (Shaw) Garden. A spotty neighborhood, with large multifamily homes predominating, Shaw has played a major role in the rehabbing movement of the past several years.

The Central West End is a cosmopolitan area adjacent to and east of Forest Park. Just 10 years ago the neighborhood was considered "transitional" and a risky area for homeowners. Today Central West End streets are alive with specialty shops, art galleries, and restaurants. Several luxury high-rise apartment buildings and elegant restored homes anchor the area. The boyhood home of poet T.S. Eliot is at 4446 Westminster Place. Playwright Tennessee Williams and poet Sara Teasdale also lived in the Central West End.

The most dramatic feature of the neighborhood is the "new" cathedral, the Cathedral of St. Louis on Lindell Boulevard at Newstead. Built between 1907 and 1914, the cathedral is a masterpiece of Romanesque architecture, and its great dome is visible for miles. The Byzantine interior has been compared favorably with the most elaborate cathedrals in Europe. Striking mosaics decorate the walls, and marble has been used ex-

tensively.

Elegant mansions line Lindell Boulevard across from Forest Park. Immediately north of Lindell are Westmoreland and Portland places, the two private streets often cited as comprising one of the most elegant neighborhoods in the world. At the turn of the century, the powerful movers and shakers of St. Louis lived here.

Between downtown and the Central West End is midtown, where Saint Louis University is located. Its Victorian Gothic DuBourg Hall and the English Gothic Church of St. Francis Xavier next door (the "college

FACING PAGE, TOP: Ten year-old Montraill Clairborne enjoys a refreshing shower in a fountain set up by the City of St. Louis Parks Department in Fox Park in south St. Louis. Photo by Wes Paz

ABOVE: Neighborhood youths practice their gymnastic skills after school on a vacant lot in the Shaw neighborhood. Photo by Wes Paz

FACING PAGE, BOTTOM: One of the most glamorous movie theaters in the nation during the 1930s and 1940s, today the "fabulous Fox" has been restored in all its palatial glory. Photo by G. Robert Bishop/HMS Group, Inc.

church") at Grand and Lindell boulevards are its most distinctive buildings.

To the north of the university is the stretch of Grand that was once the "great white way" in St. Louis. A half-dozen major theaters drew large crowds to the area. After World War II the neighborhood deteriorated and, one by one, the theaters closed. Today two have been restored and more restorations are planned. In 1968 the St. Louis Theater became Powell Hall, home of the world-renowned St. Louis Symphony Orchestra. More recently, in 1981, the 5,000-seat Fox Theater was restored to its former opulence and reopened as "the fabulous Fox." It now offers a variety of big-name performances. Nearby Sheldon Hall has a more intimate atmosphere, perfect for small ensemble performances.

There is a clear demarcation between the city of St. Louis and St. Louis County. The county has been stratified into South County, which is served by I-55 and I-44; North County, served by I-70 and I-270; and West County, neatly divided by Highway 40 (I-64).

Clayton is a focal point of business growth in West St. Louis County. It lies on a tangent to St. Louis and lies along the central corridor formed by Highway 40. Its central business district rivals that of downtown. Towering office buildings house many of the world's best-known corporate names. The nearly 2,000 firms located in Clayton include 52 *Fortune* and *Forbes* 500 corporations. The government of St. Louis County, serving a population of one million, occupies a 10-story administration building and courts complex.

Few communities in the nation possess such distinctive residential areas as Clayton. There is a variety of highly valued homes, from old brick mansions and substantial two-story homes to fashionable condominiums and apartments.

To the southwest is Webster Groves, a community rich in historic frame homes and distinguished by tree-lined streets and deep yards. For years new development has been limited in Webster Groves; the result is stability and comfort. Within the community, Webster University and Eden Seminary abut one another. On the Webster campus is the Loretto-Hilton Theatre, home of the Repertory Theatre of St. Louis ("the Rep"), an outstanding professional company, as well as the Opera Theatre of St. Louis.

Still farther west on I-44 is Kirkwood, founded in 1849 as the first commuter suburb west of the Mississippi. Built along the Missouri Pacific Railroad line, Kirkwood was intended from its beginning to be a family town, a place where children, their parents, and their grandparents could find both excitement and serenity.

Today there is a healthy mix of solid middle-class homes and retail commerce.

In Ladue, estate-type homes in the $1-million-plus range predominate in a country-club atmosphere. Ladue is the home of the prestigious St. Louis Country Club, the Bogey Golf Club, the adjacent Log Cabin Club, the Deer Creek Club, and the Old Warson Country Club. The affluent community has several outstanding private schools—John Burroughs, Country Day School, and Mary Institute.

Stone lions mark the west entrance to University City's loop, the stretch along Delmar Boulevard where government offices and shops are located. U City was named for its proximity to Washington University. It contains the most diverse ethnic mix in the area. For many years U City was the center of Jewish culture; today Russian emigres mingle with Vietnamese, Cambodians, and blacks. Cultural attractions include an art movie theater; an outstanding bookstore; St. Louis Conservatory and School for the Arts (CASA); the Craft Alliance, a unique cooperative art gallery; and the Center of Contemporary Arts (COCA).

North County is the site of Lambert International Airport and the area's largest employer, McDonnell Douglas Corporation. Several pleasant communities have developed nearby. Founded by the French in 1786 and named for the abundance of flowers growing in the region, Florissant is the most populous suburb in St. Louis

County. Like its neighboring towns, it has been settled by modest-income families. This enthusiasm has built an outstanding Civic Center in Florissant and is responsible for the annual Valley of the Flowers Festival.

At the edge of West County, Chesterfield leads the county in new-home construction. The city capitalizes on its easy access to the Highway 40 corridor in drawing new residents. Chesterfield was planned from the start to be more than a bedroom community, and today combines a variety of styles of residences with retail centers, business and industrial parks, and community services. The fast-growing Spirit of St. Louis Airport is located near Chesterfield.

At the westernmost edge of St. Louis County, the Legends is being developed by Don Breckenridge. A world-class golf course designed by Robert Trent Jones will be the centerpiece for a resort community of luxurious homes.

St. Charles County, northwest of St. Louis County, has been dubbed the "golden triangle," because its three major cities—St. Charles, St. Peters, and O'Fallon—are modern-day boom towns. Lake St. Louis, an executive-level residential community in St. Charles County, features a large man-made lake and a golf course.

FACING PAGE: The official flag of St. Louis bears the graceful *fleur-de-lis* emblem of its French heritage. Founded by merchant Pierre Laclède, the city was named for two men named Louis— Louis XV of France and his patron saint, Louis IX. Photo by Wes Paz

ABOVE: "The nation's biggest birthday party," the VP Fair makes a four-day weekend out of celebrating America's "birthday," the Fourth of July. Air shows, riverboat races, live music, and dancing draw fairgoers from around the world. Photo by Gary Bohn

Jefferson and Franklin counties are also growing fast, while still offering plenty of space for "country living," with densely wooded acreage at low prices.

Close-knit neighborhoods, urban landscapes, planned communities, family-oriented suburbs, small towns, and country living—all are found in metropolitan St. Louis and each offers residents unique opportunities for finding a life-style that fits.

31

CHAPTER THREE

An Upward Vision

"It is the longest river in the world—four thousand three hundred miles. . . . It is also the crookedest river in the world . . ."

—*Mark Twain*
Life on the Mississippi

One of St. Louis' greatest assets has always been its location on a major waterway. Another important resource is its site in the center of the country amid primarily flat or gently rolling terrain. It is easy to move goods in and out of the area in any direction, by road or rail, water or air.

The cost and speed of transporting products is a crucial factor today in competing on the world market. The ability to warehouse and distribute goods efficiently is also critically important. The St. Louis advantage is found in its multimodal facilities—readily available are excellent highways, rail networks, water and air transportation, plus transferral facilities and distribution services. This easy accessibility provides advantages in both cost and efficiency.

The city's location near the population center of the continental United States means that it is situated proximate to one-third of the nation's economic activity. In fact, St. Louis is within 500 miles of 100 metropolitan areas and nearly 80 million people.

Two classics of Americana pass each other on and above the nation's most famous river. Photo by Wes Paz

Many of the products bought by these people come through St. Louis.

For the first 100 years of its history, the Mississippi and Missouri rivers were vital links to the rest of the nation and the most significant factor in the city's economy. With the advent of railroads, the city turned its back on the river and looked west rather than east.

Today the rivers are as important to the city's growth as they were in its early years, but now because they offer an abundant and dependable supply of water for people and industry rather than for their role in transportation.

A favorite sport in St. Louis is watching the barges move along the river. Tows can consist of as many as 40 barges and require only five days to get to New Orleans. No doubt many a present-day Huckleberry Finn, enticed by the promise of adventure, would like to hop aboard.

The Mississippi River connects St. Louis with industrial centers in 15 states via the Missouri, Ohio, Illinois, and Tennessee rivers. Bulk products, extraordinarily heavy commodities, and liquids are most effectively shipped by river. These usually include coal, petroleum products, grain, chemicals, iron, and steel.

St. Louis is the northernmost point on the Mississippi River that remains ice-free and open throughout the year. Traffic north of St. Louis, on the upper Mississippi, Missouri, and Illinois rivers, is usually suspended for three months during the winter. South of St. Louis the river is unimpeded; there are no locks or dams between St. Louis and New Orleans.

The Port of Metropolitan St. Louis was organized to oversee commercial river traffic. There are 11 designated ports in the system, although not all of them are working ports. The port's jurisdiction extends 71 miles from Herculaneum, Missouri, south of St. Louis, north to Piasa Island above the Alton Dam. Both banks of the Mississippi River, as well as a portion of the Missouri and Kaskaskia rivers, are part of the port system.

Three general freight terminals have been established in the Port of Metropolitan St. Louis. Two are along the city's riverfront—the North Market Street Dock and the Rutger Street Terminal. The largest terminal, covering 77 acres, is in Granite City, Illinois, at the Tri-City Regional Port District Dock.

Robert Wydra, general manager of the Tri-City Port, emphasizes its importance to the world economy. "Seventy percent of the products that come through this port are intended for export," he says. "This is material—grain, for instance, or fertilizer—that could not be efficiently transported any other way than by water. These products come from the heart of the Midwest and are distributed throughout the world via the Mississippi River."

Coming upriver are materials intended for import, particularly automotive parts and accessories. Foreign manufacturers gladly take advantage of St. Louis' two Free Trade Zones (FTZ). In an FTZ U.S. companies are allowed to receive products from abroad and warehouse them, process them, or manufacture them into other products without paying customs duty. The duty on products in the FTZ is paid only when the product leaves the zone destined for a specific U.S. market. Anything produced in an FTZ destined for a foreign market does not have official "place of manufacture" in the U.S., and therefore is not subject to duty payments.

Companies involved in international commerce can build facilities in an FTZ to take advantage of the cost savings. A bonus at FTZ 31 (the Tri-City Port) in nearby Fenton, Missouri, is the easy accessibility to the riverside loading and unloading facilities. It also offers a 130-acre industrial park site and a large warehouse.

Plans for FTZ 31 include the development of a large distribution and industrial center which will offer banking, freight forwarding, and customs house brokerage services, as well as storage, cargo handling, and light manufacturing capabilities.

St. Louis' second FTZ, number 102, is at Bussen Quarry in south St. Louis County. The site has 150,000 square feet of storage and work space in an underground limestone quarry.

Shipments from St. Louis now can reach saltwater ports around the world without rehandling because of the development of "Lighter Aboard Ship" (LASH) containers and Seabee barges. These small barges can

FACING PAGE, TOP: For many of the Midwest's products, no other mode of shipping approaches the efficiency of water. Bulk goods and extremely heavy commodities are likely candidates for barge travel. Photo by Terry Barner/ Unicorn Stock Photos

ABOVE: St. Louis' efficient highway system offers access to any destination in the country within four days. Photo by Doug McKay/ HMS Group, Inc.

FACING PAGE, BOTTOM: Side by side again—what would the Mississippi River be without Tom Sawyer and Huck Finn? Photo by Denny Bailly/ Unicorn Stock Photos

The Eads Bridge
stretches from the
eastern shore of the
Mississippi into the
city, bringing auto-
mobiles across on its
upper deck and rail
traffic below. Its open-
ing in 1874 estab-
lished the city as a
major link between
east and west. Photo
by Doug McKay/
HMS Group, Inc.

be hoisted aboard mother ships in New Orleans for delivery to world markets. Shallow-draft "mini" vessels can load cargo at St. Louis and head directly for the Caribbean and Atlantic ports of Central America.

More than 25 million tons of freight are processed each year through the St. Louis port system—$5 billion worth. That amount exceeds the freight handled at many of the nation's ocean ports. In addition to the three general freight terminals, there are about 100 specialized terminals.

Wydra sees growth ahead for the port system, today the second busiest inland port in the nation. "The number of tons handled by the year 2000 could double," he says. "That would mean 16,000 new permanent jobs directly related to the port and another 16,000 secondary jobs." Today 15 percent of the total manufacturing employment in the region is related to the port and river transportation.

Four common carrier barge lines have home offices in St. Louis. Many private towing companies and barge lines, including liquid carriers, are headquartered in the region as well. So are four shipbuilding firms and dozens of other river-related industries— diving contractors, salvage operators, insurance carriers, and repair services, for instance. Ten shipyard repair facilities are located in or adjacent to the port. Harbor tug service is provided within a 100-mile radius of St. Louis by eight companies.

The river port system has been so successful in part because it is connected to the area's extensive rail network. The St. Louis region, including southwestern Illinois, is ranked as the second largest rail center in the nation. It provides direct freight service to 95 percent of the major population centers.

Nine trunk lines operate 26 lines and three switching lines. Among them are the Illinois Central Gulf, Burlington Northern, Union Pacific, and Santa Fe-Southern Pacific (Cotton Belt). The Alton & Southern operates St. Louis' busiest yard and has one of the nation's most modern computer-controlled operations. The rail system is complemented by eight piggyback terminals providing "trailer on flat car" (TOFC) and "container on flat car" (COFC) services. Such piggyback facilities can ship 200 to 600 trailers or containers per day.

Over 1,000 industries in the St. Louis region are served by rail, and some 100 trains move through the region daily. Yearly these trains carry more than 250,000 carloads of freight. At 13 classification yards in the region, trains are broken up and reorganized, and at "team yards" they are unloaded.

The Terminal Railroad Association (TRRA) is the oldest and largest organization of its type in the nation. It was formed in 1889 when the Missouri Pacific, the Union Pacific, the Wabash, and several other rail lines united to control rail traffic (and fees) on the Eads Bridge.

The TRRA was responsible for building the magnificent Union Station in downtown St. Louis in 1894. Today Amtrak passengers board trains at a small temporary station a few blocks south of Union Station. Construction of a new passenger station in St. Louis is now being contemplated. Amtrak provides daily

service to Kansas City, Chicago, and New Orleans.

The interstate highway system through St. Louis provides almost effortless access and interchange. Used heavily during rush hours by commuter traffic, the highways offer routes in, out, and through downtown. Travelers heading west take I-70 to Kansas City and Denver. Its eastward course goes through Indianapolis and Pittsburgh to Baltimore. I-44 begins in St. Louis and ends just southwest of Oklahoma City, paralleling the legendary Route 66.

Southbound travelers take I-55 through Memphis and Jackson, Mississippi, to New Orleans. I-55 north goes directly to Chicago. I-64, which begins (or ends) in St. Louis, takes the traveler to Louisville and Lexington, Kentucky; Charleston, West Virginia; and Richmond and Norfolk, Virginia. An outer beltway (designated I-270 in Missouri and I-255 in Illinois) rings the metropolitan area. Construction of another beltway, still farther out, is being considered.

Naturally, trucking firms take advantage of the efficient highway system. From St. Louis, overnight and first-morning shipping can be guaranteed in 25 states. Any point in the continental United States can be reached within four days.

Forty-five major truck lines have headquarters in the region, with 17 truck terminals located in or near industrial parks, railyards, and port facilities. Trucks move an average of 166,000 tons of freight in and out of St. Louis every day. About 300 general and specialized carriers transport goods locally.

Jack Staley, regional manager of Yellow Freight System, Inc., thinks the city's location is ideal. "St. Louis is a consolidation center for us," he says. "We bring in shipments from outstate Missouri and Illinois, consolidate them, and send them on to their destination very quickly."

Public transportation has been a part of St. Louis since the early nineteenth century, when horse-drawn streetcars were initiated. In 1949 the Bi-State Development Agency, a quasipublic agency, was created by Congress to develop a public transportation system that crosses state lines. Today Bi-State operates a fleet of 700 modern buses 22 hours a day, seven days a week, throughout the metropolitan region.

Beginning in August 1988 Metroliner commuter

FACING PAGE, TOP: Sergeant Joe Richardson (right) and Officer Al Adkins of the St. Louis Police Department's Mobile Reserve Unit patrol the streets of north St. Louis. Photo by Wes Paz

FACING PAGE, BOTTOM: Women firefighting trainees rest atop the main fire station downtown after a training drill. Photo by Wes Paz

BELOW: The "City of Flight" and its environs enjoy the use of several airports. Everything from light aircraft to military planes is served by world-class facilities in the area. Photo courtesy HMS Group, Inc.

buses were added. These diesel-powered buses are similar to the cross-country buses used by Greyhound, and were designed for smooth comfortable rides over long distances. Paul Ballard, Bi-State's general manager of operations, notes that these types of commuter buses have been very popular in other metropolitan areas. "We expect our ridership to grow among West County residents," he says.

Coming in 1993 is Metro Link, an electrically powered light-rail system. The 18-mile line will connect downtown St. Louis with neighborhoods and commercial centers from East St. Louis, Illinois, to Lambert-St. Louis International Airport in northern St. Louis County. The system will take advantage of

subterranean tunnels that were installed for the railroads almost 100 years ago. Twenty rail stations and a system of commuter parking lots are planned. Proposed extensions are under study.

St. Louis has been called the "City of Flight" because of its vital role in the development of aviation. Lambert-St. Louis International Airport was developed by Major Albert Bond Lambert in the 1920s and sold to the city at his cost in 1927. Lambert was also an enthusiastic backer of Charles Lindbergh's 1927 transatlantic flight, one reason Lindbergh named his airplane *The Spirit of St. Louis.*

Today Lambert Field is the eighth busiest commercial airport in the nation. It is ranked as the 10th airport in the world in number of landings and takeoffs. According to Lambert director Donald Bennett, there are over 800 commercial flights each day and approximately 250 commuter flights. Virtually any city in the continental United States can be reached from St. Louis in four hours or less.

Nine major airlines serve the airport: American, Continental, Delta, Eastern, Northwest, Southwest, TWA, United, and USAir. Four commuter lines take passengers to nearby communities: Trans World Express/ Resort Air, Air Midwest, Comair, and Prime Air.

TWA, which purchased the St. Louis-based Ozark Airlines in 1986, is by far the leading provider of airline service to and from St. Louis. Since making St. Louis a major hub in the late 1970s, TWA has increased its number of flights to and from the city each year. Today TWA has over 300 departures each day, including daily flights to London, Paris, and Frankfurt.

Over the past several years Lambert has undergone extensive and almost continuous renovation and expansion, even opening a second terminal. The airport plans to spend $130 million in the next five years on improvements and may expand still further by adding 24 more gates, bringing its total to 102.

Lambert accommodates military as well as commercial aircraft; some 12,000 military flights are logged at the field each year. General aviation, including corporate aircraft, also takes advantage of Lambert's runways, but most noncommercial flights are directed to one of the area's other 15 airfields.

The largest and fastest-growing airport outside of Lambert is Spirit of St. Louis Airport in West County near Chesterfield. Covering 11,000 acres of land, the airport accommodates business aircraft with 30 to 40 flights daily. Most take off in the morning and return in the evening. Since many executives live in West County, this schedule is especially convenient.

Ninety-five corporate jets are hangared at the field, which is owned and operated by St. Louis County. Among the corporate operators are Anheuser-Busch, Monsanto, Ralston Purina, and Southwestern Bell.

Spirit director Dick Hrabko is enthusiastic about the future of the airport. "We have 600 acres that have not yet been developed, so we have plenty of room to expand," he says. "It has been proved that it is more efficient for a corporation to operate its own jet than to put executives through the inconveniences of commercial flight. It saves time and money."

A 1,000-acre industrial park is adjacent to Spirit. At the field are several fixed-based operators, flight schools, and air taxi services. The FAA maintains a highly sophisticated automated flight service station, providing weather information and in-flight communications within a 400-mile radius. A public golf course is being developed adjacent to the airport.

Second to Spirit in number of general aviation flights daily is St. Louis Downtown-Parks Airport. Located in Cahokia, Illinois, just across the Mississippi River from downtown, it is home to approximately 200 aircraft and encompasses a 200-acre business park. The airport, operated by the Bi-State Development Agency, is near the campus of Parks College of Saint Louis University, a highly regarded school that offers programs in all phases of aviation technology.

In Madison County, Illinois, not far from the Tri-City Port, is St. Louis Regional Airport, the third busiest general aviation field. Other general aviation airports on the Missouri side of the metropolitan area include Weiss, Creve Coeur, St. Charles, and Wentzville.

The East-West Gateway Coordinating Council, the major planning body in the bi-state area, recently released its heliport system plan, which is to go into effect during the 1990s.

The fastest-growing category of helicopter use is emergency medical service and patient transfer. The Medical Air Rescue Corps and Saint Louis University

Medical Center operate several helicopters for such purposes. Electronic news gathering, law enforcement, sightseeing, construction (" heavy lift" operations), military, and business transportation are other uses that keep helicopters busy.

At least 15 new heliports are scheduled to be developed during the next 15 years. A downtown public heliport will act as the hub of the system and eventually will be used for city-to-city passenger transport.

The economic impact on the St. Louis area of all forms of transportation is in the billions annually. Manufacturers are wholly dependent on the smooth functioning of the transportation system and, in fact, many have located their firms here because of its dependability and efficiency.

Despite the ribbons of concrete expressways and the growing air traffic, the mystique of St. Louis transportation is still the river. Mark Twain grew up with the Mississippi River in his front yard and couldn't wait to travel on it. Poet T.S. Eliot called it "a strong, brown god." The river defines St. Louis, nurtures it, and enriches it. The city will continue to grow as long as the Mississippi "keeps on rolling along."

CHAPTER FOUR

A Soaring Structure

"First in booze, first in shoes, and last in the American League."

—Old saying

Because St. Louis was founded as a center for trade, its manufacturing capabilities were exploited later than those of many cities. In 1860, on the eve of the Civil War, the city was seventh in the nation in value of products manufactured, sixth in the number of manufacturing firms, and ninth in payrolls. Food processing and meat packing were the dominant industries.

Today St. Louis is the nation's 11th largest manufacturing center and the 11th largest labor market. Food processing is still an integral part of the economy, but manufacturing has greatly diversified and now the region's 4,000 plants produce a variety of brand names that are recognized all over the world.

Throughout the late nineteenth and early twentieth centuries, St. Louis was proud of being a "smokestack" town. Smokey air meant business was booming. But the poor quality of air became a serious

Students at Tarkio College train to become cable television installers. St. Louis' highly skilled work force is an indispensable asset to its industrial vigor. Photo by Gary Bohn

42

problem in the 1920s and 1930s, and in 1940 a stiff smoke-abatement law was enacted which prohibited the burning of soft coal. Since then the city's air has been carefully monitored and recent air pollution ordinances have forced most of the old smokestack industries to move from the riverfront area to new facilities in industrial parks.

There are still industrial sites available in the St. Louis region, although the land is being absorbed at the rate of 170 acres per year. Industrial vacancy rates have remained fairly constant at around 4.5 percent—slightly below the national average. Today manufacturing firms are spread out throughout the region, mostly located in landscaped, attractive buildings almost indistinguishable from college campuses. Abatement of noise, air, and water pollution has been taken seriously and the result is a new style of community-aware industrial management.

Bob Kelley, head of the St. Louis Labor Council, sees the trend as a healthy one for the community and for labor. "The major issue facing labor unions today is being assured of safe working conditions, and that includes clean air and less noise," he says. He points out that only 40 years ago, most union members headed downtown to work in the garment district or in the foundries and factories along the riverfront. "Today most workers go west, even west of Highway 270—that's where the plants are."

The work force in the St. Louis region today encompasses more than 1.2 million people. About 21 percent, or 225,600 workers, are employed in manufacturing. Skills availability is rated as good in the region due to the concentration of industries such as aircraft, automobiles, fabricated metals, food, chemicals, nonelectrical machinery, and primary metals. These categories make up two-thirds of the manufacturing work force.

Kelley says that union workers in the St. Louis region are both highly skilled and highly motivated to produce quality work—and business leaders agree. More than 50 vocational, industrial, and trade schools in the area offer first-rate electronic, engineering, and applied technology programs. Quit rates in the area are far below the national average. Unemployment rates over the last several years have ranged between 5 and 11 percent.

At one time St. Louis was known for the frequency and duration of its strikes, but within the last 15 years the region has seen a substantial improvement in labor-

ABOVE: Labor relations have improved greatly in recent times. For instance, over the past nine years the proportion of St. Louis workers who have been involved in work stoppages has been substantially lower than the national average. Photo by Gary Bohn

TOP: A vendor displays her goods at the Soulard Farmer's Market. Photo by Wes Paz

FACING AND FOLLOWING PAGE: One of St. Louis industry's traditional leaders, today Anheuser-Busch is one of the five largest employers in the region. Photos courtesy HMS Group, Inc.

management relations. Over a recent nine-year span covering three contract periods, the proportion of workers involved in stoppages due to labor-management disputes averaged 10 percent below the U.S. rate. The proportion of locally negotiated contracts occurring without strikes has been well over 90 percent.

Outstanding progress has been made in the construction industry by two labor-management committees—PRIDE (Productivity and Responsibility Increase Development and Employment) in the Missouri counties and Image in the Illinois counties. These programs have resulted in the virtual elimination of worker-days lost due to strikes. The New Spirit of St. Louis labor-management committee is applying the same cooperative concepts to labor relations in manufacturing, retailing, distribution, and other unionized businesses.

The largest employers in the region today are McDonnell Douglas Aircraft, Monsanto Company, Chrysler Corporation, Emerson Electric, and Anheuser-Busch. Together these five companies employ some 60,000 workers locally. Even more important to the city's economy, each has spawned dozens of ancillary industries that keep the giants supplied with important parts and services.

St. Louis is a frequent choice for the location of regional and national corporate headquarters. In fact, it is ranked third nationally in the number of headquarters of *Fortune*'s top 100 industrial firms. Three hundred and twenty *Fortune* 500 companies have offices in the region. The most frequent reasons given for choosing St. Louis as a headquarters city are its location, excellent transportation system, affordability, and outstanding quality of life.

Shoes and beer have long been almost synonymous with St. Louis. Brown Shoe, a part of the Brown Group, headquartered in Clayton, is the leading manufacturer of branded footwear in the United States. Popular brands include Life Stride, Naturalizer, Buster Brown, Connie, and Fanfare shoes. Interco is another major producer of shoes and apparel. Its best-known shoe brands include Converse and Florsheim. Another major company, Kellwood, manufactures apparel and home fashions, among them most of the private label fashions sold in Sears stores.

For years the automotive industry was an important part of the city's economy. St. Louis factories assembled more motor vehicles than any city in the nation except Detroit. Robotics at General Motors, Ford, and Chrysler plants have become national models of efficiency.

The chemical industry employs nearly 4 percent of the manufacturing work force. Monsanto, an inter-

ABOVE: Mallinckrodt, Inc., has been a part of St. Louis industry for more than a century. Its original plant dates to 1867 and now occupies 50 acres near the downtown area. A vast array of specialty chemicals are manufactured here for customers around the world. Photo by Doug McKay/ HMS Group, Inc.

FACING PAGE, LEFT: Robotics and other high-tech fields are nurtured by business and educational leaders, making St. Louis a growing center for such industries. Here, a robot carries out automated welding at a St. Louis automobile plant. Photo courtesy HMS Group, Inc.

FACING PAGE, RIGHT: Computer software and information processing are an integral part of St. Louis' forward-looking industrial scene. Photo by Ferguson & Katzman/ HMS Group, Inc.

national company with sales of $7.6 billion, develops, makes, and markets chemical and agricultural products, pharmaceuticals, plastics, and electronic materials. Its best-known product today is probably Nutra-Sweet, the artificial sweetener. Sigma-Aldrich, Mallinckrodt, and Petrolite are other major chemical companies. Twenty-five area firms produce drugs, including Norcliff-Thayer, which makes the ubiquitous Tums.

St. Louis is rapidly becoming a center for high-tech industries—firms that have an above-average ratio of research and development expenditures to sales. While 29.2 percent of manufacturing firms across the nation are considered high tech, 37.9 percent of St. Louis manufacturing firms are so designated. Approximately 84,000 people in St. Louis, or 7.5 percent of the nonagricultural labor force, are employed by high-tech industries (The national average is 5.4 percent). These include engineers, computer specialists, scientists, technicians, and health specialists.

St. Louis leaders are committed to fostering the development of technology-oriented industries. The St. Louis Technology Center, funded in part by the state of Missouri, was created by business leaders in cooperation with area universities and colleges to encourage the technological application of scientific research. The center operates the New Business Incubator, which encourages the growth of new high-tech businesses by providing essential support services to the entrepreneur.

The dozens of new businesses launched by the center are in the areas of biotechnology, robotics, computer software, electronics, and life sciences. Gene Boesch, managing director of the center, points out that St. Louis has always had a base of technological manufacturing firms, but within the last 10 years the growth of such firms has accelerated. "It's an exciting time for the

center," he says. "Its growth has exceeded our expectations. More and more young engineers and scientists are becoming involved in the research and development of new products. The companies that we help them start create new jobs for the area."

Missouri Research Park is currently being developed in Weldon Spring by the University of Missouri. This park will house high-tech companies in a campus environment.

A new "old" high-tech company is Southwestern Bell Technology Resource, a division of Southwestern Bell Telephone. Vice president Peter Jackson says that the health of the region's economy depends on the efficient communication of knowledge—information processing. "Our labs are developing new technology resources that will affect the future of business and of society as a whole. New ideas are encouraged. Tomorrow's telephone networks will bring computerized catalogs, encyclopedias, stock market reports—you name it. All of us will be able to be in touch with the world of information."

Monsanto recently opened a 210-acre Life Science Center in suburban St. Louis County. About 1,000 scientists and technicians are employed there in research on

agriculture, nutrition chemicals, and health care. Its most glamorous objective is the development of genetic engineering. Monsanto scientists recently achieved a breakthrough in inserting a new genetic trait (via recombinant DNA) into a plant cell, then regenerating the plant and subsequent generations. Monsanto's annual Science Fair, cosponsored by the *Post-Dispatch*, encourages school-age youngsters to develop an interest in science.

Food processing plants have also turned high tech. Anheuser-Busch, in conjunction with Interferon Sciences, Inc., has produced interferon and related biological products through the use of genetic engineering and yeast fermentation. Ralston Purina, the world's largest producer of animal feeds (Puppy Chow and Meow Mix, for instance), maintains research facilities for work on animal nutrition and in the area of isolating proteins for human nutrition. Pet, Inc., has pioneered in food preservation for years. Today it is testing gamma radiation to sterilize food without heat.

A major market for high-tech industries is the federal government and specifically the Department of Defense. Harold Guller, president of Essex Industries, a leading supplier of high-tech defense products, sees the relationship between St. Louis and the Defense Department as a healthy one. "Most of the time it works well," he says. "And the number of contracts coming to this area is likely to grow."

McDonnell Douglas Aircraft designs and assembles combat aircraft for the air force, navy, marines, and several foreign nations, as well as working to convert military planes to peacetime use. The company also received major contracts for space vehicles and equipment. McDonnell Douglas Astronautics produces antiship cruise missiles. The company's $35-million Microelectronics Center turns out microchips with circuits 50 to 100 times thinner than a human hair. McDonnell Douglas Electronics makes flight simulators

TOP: The defense industry is a vigorous component in St. Louis' high-tech community. McDonnell Douglas is a major player in the design and manufacture of military aircraft, as well as such exciting peacetime technologies as space vehicles and artificial intelligence. Photo by Doug McKay/ HMS Group, Inc.

ABOVE: Chris Brecht applies "dope" to the fabric covering of a Cessna 140 wing at Potosi Aviation at Dauster Field. Photo by Wes Paz

FACING PAGE: Aggressive economic development efforts, strong human and natural resources, and a diverse mix of industries combine to make St. Louis a rich center of opportunity. Photo by Gary Bohn

and other aerospace electronics, while McDonnell Douglas Information Systems operates the world's largest computer center. A new project that McDonnell Douglas has taken on with Washington University is the exploration of artificial intelligence.

The headquarters for General Dynamics is in St. Louis, although its manufacturing facilities are not. The company, a giant in the defense industry, supplies aircraft, missiles, submarines, space systems, and computer systems for the military.

Emerson Electric, with sales of $6.2 billion, is one of the largest electronics companies in the nation. It manufactures a wide range of electrical and electronic products and systems for commercial and industrial use, consumer use, and defense use. Harvard Industries, a relatively new *Fortune* 500 company, manufactures engineered products for the automotive, aerospace, and defense industries.

An abundant supply of water is available to St. Louis industries from three rivers—the Mississippi, Missouri, and Meramec. The combined flow of these rivers is 100 times the average daily demand of the area. Purified water and well water are available from private and municipal systems.

Sewage is handled by municipalities, private companies, and the areawide Metropolitan St. Louis Sewer District. Through its three major treatment plants, the MSD serves the major portion of the city and county of St. Louis. Water control boards monitor the disposal of treated industrial wastes into open streams and impounded waters.

Union Electric Company provides electricity for the Missouri portion of the St. Louis metropolitan area. It has never experienced a brownout or blackout from lack of power, and even supplies a regional organization with its excess power supply. The company is actively pursuing increased industrial loads and has recently opened a new nuclear plant with a 1.15-million-kilowatt unit in Calloway County, west of the St. Louis region.

Tremendous coal deposits are found in the Illinois-Missouri area. About two-thirds of the 137 billion tons of coal in Illinois lie within 125 miles of St. Louis. Coal is also mined in three Missouri counties within a 125-mile radius of the city. Much of this coal can be successfully reached using surface techniques.

Oil is also readily available in the St. Louis region. Fifty-eight distribution companies are located here. Shell Oil's petroleum refinery in Wood River, Illinois, has a capacity of 300,000 barrels per day and is one of the largest refineries in the nation.

Laclede Gas Company furnishes natural gas for residential, commercial, and industrial customers in the region. It is a leading participant in a successful gas exploration program that began in 1972 and has resulted in the development of dedicated wells in Texas, Louisiana, and Oklahoma. Mississippi River Transmission Company transports natural gas to the St. Louis region from fields in east Texas and north Louisiana.

The taxing structure in the St. Louis region is generally considered advantageous for manufacturers. The state of Missouri gives corporate income tax credit for new facilities, and tax rates on real property are competitive with other metropolitan areas. There is no inventory tax.

Less than 6 percent of Missouri's revenue is derived from corporate income taxes. More than half of the state's revenue comes from sales taxes and gross receipt taxes. Another 8.7 percent comes from licenses and fees.

A Missouri-based company usually has a lower corporate tax bill than it would have in most other states. Missouri is one of only five states that allow federal income tax payments to be deducted before computing taxable income. Using this deduction, a corporation with a taxable income of one million dollars would have an effective tax rate of approximately 3.3 percent—lower than all but one of the 46 states imposing a corporate income tax.

The city of St. Louis levies a one-percent tax on the net income of businesses in the city. There are no deductions. All city residents and those working in the city also pay a one-percent income tax. This is balanced by a low property tax.

Missouri provides assistance for construction of new facilities through revenue bonds issued by local industrial development corporations. These tax-exempt bonds may be issued without referendum at below-market interest rates. St. Louis city's Planned Industrial Expansion Authority may issue industrial revenue bonds and assist in acquiring property for redevelopment through the city's power of eminent domain.

All levels of government in Missouri, from the state capital of Jefferson City to the counties, cities, and municipalities involved, are aggressively seeking economic development and offer powerful incentives to businesses moving into the area. Five major economic development organizations teamed up in 1987 to promote an "I'm Sold on St. Louis" campaign, which is aimed at bringing new industry to the region. So far, according to a recent *Commerce* magazine article, it's working. Nearly 40,000 jobs have been added to the region since the campaign began.

CHAPTER FIVE

The Infrastructure

"Knowledge—Zzzzzp! Money—Zzzzzp! Power—Zzzzzp! That's the cycle democracy is built on!"

—Tennessee Williams
The Glass Menagerie

St. Louis offers its business community—from mom-and-pop grocery stores to international corporations—a wide range of support services. These include financial and legal networks, clerical and management personnel pools, and top-flight sales promotion and advertising.

The ease with which money is available is crucial to any business, and the banking industry in St. Louis is highly competitive, both inside and outside the region. Because the city is the world headquarters for several major international corporations, its banks must provide the most sophisticated banking techniques offered anywhere in the world. Major St. Louis banks fit comfortably into the network of U.S. and foreign financial institutions serving megacorporations, offering multilingual personnel and a full range of import-export services.

St. Louis is the headquarters for the eighth Federal Reserve District, which covers

The annual Veiled Prophet Fair draws crowds from throughout the region. Among other things, attendees can enjoy a spectacular air show. Photo by Gary Bohn

southern Illinois, southern Indiana, western Tennessee, western Kentucky, all of Arkansas, and the eastern two-thirds of Missouri. The "Fed" keeps a tight rein on the money supply in the district and is in constant contact with other district headquarters.

St. Louis banks are prepared to participate in major financial transactions, whether in real estate or in the buying and selling of corporations. Donald Lasater, the recently retired chief executive officer of Mercantile Bank, says, "St. Louis banking offers a great deal of flexibility. We can quickly adapt to market conditions."

The largest bank in the region is Boatmen's Bank, with assets of more than $14 billion. It is also the oldest bank west of the Mississippi. Chartered in 1847 to provide a savings institution for "the boatmen and other industrious classes" of the city, Boatmen's weathered the turbulent economic climate of the Civil War and is credited with stimulating the construction of railroads during the 1860s.

Boatmen's Bancshares recently acquired Centerre Bank of St. Louis as well as Centerre Trust Company, and is now considered a "superregional" bank because it operates in Illinois and Tennessee, in addition to its banking centers throughout Missouri. Andrew Craig, Boatmen's new chief executive, is determined to boost the bank's profit margins to one percent of assets within the next few years.

Craig emphasized in a recent *Commerce* magazine interview that, because of the relative stability, security, and constant growth of the Midwest economy, St. Louis is an ideal place for businesses to locate. "Our ability to keep and attract private enterprise to this region," he said, "is strongly affected by the quality of life here." St. Louis banks have traditionally contributed heavily to the city's cultural institutions.

Mercantile Bancorporation, with assets of nearly $7 billion, is the second largest bank in the region. The Merc was the key to St. Louis' turnaround in the 1970s. By refusing to leave the downtown area and by providing financing for crucial projects, the bank proved its commitment to the city's growth.

Both Boatmen's and Mercantile banks have established a strong presence in Kansas City. The next two largest banks in St. Louis, Commerce Bank and United Missouri Bank, are both headquartered in Kansas City.

The mortgage business in St. Louis is as competitive as banking. Approximately 300 mortgage lenders in the area vie for the estimated lending potential of $1.75 billion. Citicorp, the nation's largest financial services company, recently moved its national mortgage division to St. Louis. Today Citicorp's local market share is about 5 percent. It is also the number-one issuer of "jumbo loans," those in the $200,000-plus range.

While the giant financial institutions work easily with *Fortune* 500 companies, scores of smaller, independent banks specialize in services to small and midsized businesses. The most active in this area are Landmark Bancshares, Mark Twain Bancshares, and Southside Bancshares. Several Illinois banks also participate in the region's financial network.

Missouri-based savings and loan institutions have not realized the same growth that banks have. For the last few years, as national attention has been focused on poorly managed savings and loans, depositors have turned elsewhere seeking a large return on their money and have even withdrawn substantial amounts from the associations.

Several local brokerage houses dominate the stock and bond market. The rapidly growing A.G. Edwards & Sons is headquartered near downtown. Edward D. Jones & Co., which developed a unique approach by appealing to the small investor in small-town America, has built a sprawling campus in West County for its headquarters. Stifel, Nicolaus & Co. is

a widely respected national brokerage firm whose home office is in St. Louis.

Large-scale investors can find a 30- to 50-percent return on investments through venture capital projects. As reported in a recent *Commerce* article, Richard Ford of Gateway Venture Partners sees the future of venture capitalism as bright in the St. Louis region. "The venture capital industry has gained the degree of respectability from professional investors necessary to ensure its long-term viability," he said.

The insurance industry is another important part of

FACING PAGE: In an effort to promote the growing convention business in the city, the Cervantes Convention and Exhibition Center is currently being expanded. Photo by James Blank

ABOVE: As St. Louis has grown, so too has the demand for professional services. The city maintains some of the highest quality police, fire, and correctional facilities nationwide, making it one of America's safest cities. Photo by Wes Paz

Retail trade is an important part of the St. Louis economy. This is the Marketplace in Historic Union Station. Photo by James Blank

"The world created by the mall itself and by the stores within is a world of fantasy, an incredibly beautiful place." The truth in these words is reflected in the lavish yet functional interior of Northwest Plaza. Photo by G. Robert Bishop/ HMS Group, Inc.

the region's financial network. Experts predict that the 1990s will see an increase in competition among insurance companies, with banking and investment firms offering insurance programs as well.

General American Life Insurance Company is the region's largest insurance firm, with assets of almost $4.5 billion. Its striking national headquarters has become a downtown landmark, and the company is a strong supporter of civic projects through its dynamic chief executive officer, Edward Trusheim.

Accounting firms today do much more than keep the books. Management consulting services and information systems services have grown as auditing and tax services have become computerized. Today accounting firms are required to be creative as well as detail-oriented and thoroughgoing.

Peat Marwick Main & Co., Arthur Anderson, Ernst & Young, and Price Waterhouse have large regional offices in St. Louis. The St. Louis office of Ernst & Young specializes in financial counseling for clients involved in foreign investments and international trade.

St. Louis also is a major legal center, home of the Eighth Circuit U.S. Court of Appeals, as well as the federal district court for Eastern Missouri. Some 5,300 members of the Missouri bar practice in the city and county. In residence are 13 of the 18 arbitrators in Missouri, all members of the National Academy. Missouri trial level and appellate courts are located in downtown St. Louis and in Clayton.

St. Louis is safer than the average American city in terms of property and violent crime. The region is well policed, and the police have a reputation for being responsive and helpful. In St. Louis County, 63 municipal police departments and the county police patrol the area. In the city, there are 3.96 officers per 1,000 residents, almost twice the national average. The city of St. Louis operates a jail and workhouse; the county has a correctional center with a work release program so successful that it has become a national model.

The two largest law firms in the city are Bryan, Cave, McPheeters & McRoberts and Thompson & Mitchell, employing over 400 attorneys between them. Both specialize in corporate law and both have offices in Washington, D.C., and elsewhere. Thompson & Mitchell has built a substantial practice in maritime law and laws affecting international trade.

The in-house legal staffs of the region's major corporations are also an important part of the legal community, and often have developed specialties unique to their firms. For instance, some attorneys for Monsanto and Ralston Purina are experts in the fields of trademark and patent law.

For businesses that have products or services to sell, the St. Louis region has hundreds of advertising agencies, ranging from two-person shoestring offices to billion-dollar subsidiaries of multinational agencies. St. Louis is ranked ninth in advertising billings. The largest agency in the region—also the fifth largest in the nation and the 10th largest in the world—is D'Arcy Masius Benton & Bowles, which opened in 1906 when the advertising industry was in its infancy.

Maritz, Inc., offers unique programs for business. During the 1950s the company evolved into a sales motivation firm. Calling itself a "performance improvement company," today Maritz Motivation Co. develops sales programs and suggests costcutting for major corporations. Through its Maritz Travel division, it arranges travel for sales incentive programs and for corporate clients.

Maritz Communications has its own production facilities for developing film, slide, and audiovisual programs for clients. Its newest division, Maritz Performance Improvement Training Division, offers training programs for a variety of technical jobs.

St. Louis business leaders are generally proud of the fact that office salaries in the region, including those for electronic data processing personnel, are below the national average and are lower than in most other large metropolitan areas. (The low cost of living in the region keeps salaries fairly constant.) Skilled clerical personnel are plentiful and the area's many business schools turn out hundreds of well-trained job applicants each year.

Dozens of organizations are geared toward the needs of businesspeople. The most comprehensive is the Regional Commerce and Growth Association, formerly the Chamber of Commerce. The RCGA aggressively seeks new businesses for the region, particularly manufacturing firms, and supports those already established with informational seminars, publications, and advocacy programs. The RCGA is also committed to maintaining a high quality of life in the region and supports most educational and cultural projects.

Branches of virtually every professional organization in the nation are found in St. Louis, and the city is the national headquarters for the American Association of Orthodontists, American Optometric Association, American Soybean Association, Catholic Health Association, International Council for Small Business, and Society of Professional Archaeologists, among many other similar associations.

Because of its central location and excellent convention facilities, St. Louis is often chosen as a convention site for professional and trade organizations. Cervantes Convention and Exhibition Center, located on the north edge of the central business district, is now being expanded. The supply of hotel and motel rooms is expected to keep pace with the demand.

Two major publications circulate especially to the business community. The *St. Louis Business Journal,* a weekly tabloid, offers news, features, advice, and commentary. The RCGA's *Commerce* is a slick monthly magazine that addresses issues of interest to businesspeople, giving readers information about the eco-

nomic growth of the region as well as profiles of business leaders. The *St. Louis Post-Dispatch* offers a special business supplement, "Business Plus," once a week in addition to its regular business page.

Hundreds of computer centers, office supply stores, and business machine sales offices are situated in the region. Commercial real estate companies, office design firms, and design-and-build construction companies stand ready to give both large and small businesses the facilities they need.

Mail service in the region is bolstered by the presence of a USPS bulk mail center and a regional mail classification center. St. Louis is also a United Parcel Service hub location, and dozens more delivery services are located here.

Retail trade is an important part of the St. Louis regional economy. Indeed, across the nation shopping has become both an art and a science, a pleasure for aesthetes and bargain hunters alike. The most difficult problem facing shoppers today is choosing among the great number of options available—between specialty shops and discount centers, between downtown department stores and suburban malls.

In the St. Louis region retail trade totals $17.2 billion a year. Since 1980 the local compound annual growth rate of 10 percent has averaged considerably above the U.S. rate of 7 percent. Even after allowing for price increases, St. Louis retail sales grew by a solid 6 percent per year between 1980 and 1990.

The St. Louis region is a major market. It is 11th in the nation in population and has a total personal income of $47 billion. The median household in the region is 12 percent more affluent than the national median, and per-capita incomes are expected to keep pace with those across the U.S.

It is anticipated that the next decade will show major gains in the retailing industry as the demand for consumer goods continues. Of the millions spent for retail goods in the St. Louis region, approximately one-fourth goes for automobiles and gasoline, and slightly less for food. General merchandise accounts for one-eighth of the total, and lesser percentages are accorded to eating and drinking establishments, furniture, and drugs.

The oldest department store in the St. Louis area is Famous-Barr, which is almost synonymous with St. Louis. Today part of the international May Company, the store was founded as a small men's clothing shop in 1870. It was given the name the Famous Company, according to legend, when a rural customer said, "All the farmers out yonder are talking about this place it's

gittin' to be quite famous."

Famous purchased the William Barr Company in 1911, and the new company built a large downtown department store. An afternoon spent shopping at Famous-Barr, after lunch in its elegant tea room, quickly became part of St. Louis culture. In 1948 the store opened a branch in Clayton, and the successful development of suburban shopping centers was assured.

Today the May Company, which operates Venture Stores throughout the nation, is the region's second largest employer and has sales over $10 billion.

Twenty major shopping malls can be found in the St. Louis region today and all are being constantly upgraded to provide shoppers with the most convenient, attractive, and exciting shopping possible. Events, from high-school choir concerts to the arrival of television personalities, are frequently scheduled, and theme weekends with art and cultural exhibits draw visitors from hundreds of miles.

Bruce Schrier, creative director of Worth Stores Corporation, based in St. Louis, says of the trend toward using marble and granite, glass and oak in malls, "The world created by the mall itself and by the stores within is a world of fantasy, an incredibly beautiful place." Landscaped interior "boulevards" have replaced ordinary hallways, and window displays for individual shops are more inviting than ever.

One of the most interesting malls in the region is St. Louis Centre, which opened in the mid-1980s. An innovative "vertical mall," it is located in the center of downtown between Famous-Barr and Dillard's department stores. With convenient parking and a host of specialty shops, St. Louis Centre has been more successful than its developers dared to hope. It is bringing thousands of shoppers downtown after years of heading for suburban malls.

Also downtown is Union Station, which has been converted from a major railroad depot into a mall with boutiques for souvenir hunters, excellent restaurants, and snack shops.

Perhaps the favorite malls for the discriminating shopper would be the Galleria in Clayton and Plaza Frontenac in the town of Frontenac. Both have shops that cater to those with expensive tastes. Neiman-Marcus and Saks Fifth Avenue are located at Plaza Frontenac, as well as dozens of elegant boutiques.

Those looking for mid-priced department stores will find them at South County Center, the Ultra Mall in Crestwood, West County Center, Northwest Plaza, and the Chesterfield Mall in Missouri, and at St. Clair Square and Alton Square in Illinois.

Distinctive shopping neighborhoods are found in the Central West End, where unusual specialty shops predominate, and along the Cherokee strip in South St. Louis, which is lined with antique and "junque" shops. The Farmers' Market in Soulard, a mile south of downtown, is noted for its fresh produce and variety meats.

Demographics indicate that the 35-to-44 age group is growing rapidly in the St. Louis region. The economic result of this growth will be a geometric increase in retail trade, as these are the peak buying years. St. Louis retailers are ready to meet the demand.

CHAPTER SIX

Design for Living

"All is but the mirror of a mighty mind."

—William Marion Reedy
"The Mirror"

As soon as Missouri was declared a U.S. territory in 1812, land was set aside for the development of public schools. Because of political infighting, however, it was not until 1838 that the first public school bell rang. Before that time private schools and tutors educated the city's children. In 1878 St. Louis was the home of the first public school kindergarten in the nation, established by Susan Blow.

Today some 360,000 children attend public schools in the St. Louis region, and 82,000 children attend private or parochial schools. The latter are primarily Catholic and Lutheran.

The region's public schools, spread out over 109 districts in two states, vary widely in quality and goals. Missouri school districts follow a traditional kindergarten through 12th grade pattern. The St. Louis city school district has the largest enrollment of any district in the area, with more than 45,000 students. St. Louis County has three times as many students, but divides

Long evening shadows are cast upon the walls of Columbia School by three youths trying out their new Christmas Skates.

TOP: St. Louis' children have many educational options, from public magnet schools through a wide array of nearby colleges and universities. Photo by Wes Paz

ABOVE: A youngster takes a break during Sunday School classes at the Islamic Center near the St. Louis University campus. Photo by Wes Paz

FACING PAGE: If a good education is one's portal to the finer things of life, St. Louis' young people need not find themselves excluded. This couple at the *Fleur de Lis* debutante ball might be students of St. Louis Medical School, Parks College of Aviation, or any number of other respected institutions. Photo by Wes Paz

them up into 24 districts.

The Special School District in St. Louis County serves handicapped and vocational students. Some handicapped children attend very small classes—with a 3-to-1 pupil-teacher ratio—in buildings that have been architecturally modified; as many as possible are mainstreamed into regular schools. The Special School District holds speech and hearing screenings each year for students enrolled in county schools. Such evaluations often forestall potential behavior problems.

A nationally known school for hearing impaired children in the St. Louis area is Central Institute for the Deaf. CID's teaching techniques and research programs have won world renown. The Missouri School for the Blind and the Elias Michael School for the orthopedically handicapped are also in the city. Exceptionally bright children may attend the Mark Twain Institute, where the average IQ of students is 136.8.

As elsewhere in the nation, regional school expenditures are linked to property tax revenues. The wealthiest school district in the area is Clayton, with an expenditure of more than $6,000 per child. Most West County public schools are almost as well off.

The state of Missouri guarantees a minimum expenditure level per pupil, even in the poorest districts, but the formula to ensure this figure is complex and bureaucracy has caused many delays in the program's implementation. Nonetheless, the expenditure per pupil in the region is higher than the national average.

The teaching staff in the St. Louis region is generally considered good. Most are trained locally, at Harris-Stowe Teachers College, the University of Missouri at St. Louis, or Saint Louis University. Teachers have an average of 14 years experience and a significant number have master's degrees. The pupil-teacher ratio is well below the national average for public elementary and secondary schools in the area. The high school dropout rate in the city of St. Louis is about 10 percent; in the county it is less than 5 percent.

The most difficult problem that the school systems in the city and county of St. Louis face is one they have been struggling with since 1954—racial integration. The voluntary desegregation plan currently under way is the largest of its kind in the nation. Students can transfer from city to county schools or from county to

two military academies, and schools stressing foreign languages, the classics, and health careers.

"The nation's urban school systems have brought particularly perplexing dilemmas," says School Superintendent Jerome B. Jones. "Today a full renovation program—the largest of its kind in the nation—is taking place in the St. Louis public school system. It involves comprehensive repairs for more than 100 of our buildings, plus construction of several completely new schools and numerous classroom and multipurpose additions.

"We are excited about the achievements of our students on recent tests and predict even more progress in the years to come."

Schools in the St. Louis region consistently earn top national honors. Recently seven local elementary schools were cited for excellence by the U.S. Department of Education and the Council for American Private Education. Four local junior and senior high schools also earned national honors awarded by the U.S. Department of Education. Parkway West and Horton-Watkins (Ladue School District) are consistently rated as two of the best public high schools in the nation.

Scholastic Aptitude Test (SAT) and American College Test (ACT) scores in the west suburban areas are above the national norms, and there is a high ratio of graduating seniors going on to college.

Outstanding college preparatory schools in the region are the private, nonsectarian John Burroughs, Mary Institute, and St. Louis Country Day, and the parochial Chaminade, Christian Brothers College, Cor Jesu Academy, DeSmet, Priory, and Saint Louis University High School.

The St. Louis region is fortunate to have a rich variety of higher education resources in research, training, and liberal arts. Thirty-five such institutions are found in the area, ranging from major universities to specialized four-year colleges, medical, law, and theological schools, and two-year community colleges. Within a

city schools. Predominately white county schools are able to increase their minority populations to 25 percent through busing. White county students are encouraged to attend city magnet schools, which offer a variety of programs not found in traditional county schools.

There are now several magnet schools for the visual and performing arts, an academy of math and science,

few hours' drive are the main campus of the University of Missouri (Columbia), Southern Illinois University (Carbondale), and the University of Illinois (Champaign-Urbana).

The oldest university in the region is Saint Louis University, a Jesuit institution founded in 1818. It has an urban campus located three miles west of downtown, and its presence has contributed greatly to the renaissance of midtown. Saint Louis University Medical School, with its university hospitals complex, is located one mile south of the main campus.

One component of SLU is Parks College, which is just east of St. Louis in Cahokia, Illinois. Parks College has played an important role in the history of aviation and today offers a wide range of degrees relating to aviation technology.

Washington University in St. Louis is ranked among the leading institutions in the nation in science, engineering, and economics. Its faculty shines with well-known scholars in every discipline, and English professor Howard Nemerov was recently named U.S. poet laureate.

Wash U is private and nondenominational, and has a total endowment of more than one billion dollars—the 10th largest in the nation. The university has worked closely with corporations in scientific research. Monsanto Co. recently committed $62 million to Wash U for research in genetics and microbiology.

The Wash U Medical School is in the Central West End, surrounded by major hospitals. Barnes Hospital, the school's main teaching facility, is famed for its innovative health care and superior technology. It has been ranked as one of the top five hospitals in the nation.

The University of Missouri at St. Louis is the youngest campus of the oldest state university west of the Mississippi. Less than 30 years old, UMSL has a campus population of 12,000 and eight schools. Lowe MacLean, vice chancellor for student affairs, says that UMSL is an "academic bridge" because it provides tutoring, mentoring, and enrichment at the high school level to prepare students for college.

"All academically talented young people in our area must be educated to their full potential if we are to retain a competitive edge on the economic front," MacLean wrote in a recent *Post-Dispatch* feature. In 1986 UMSL's chancellor, Marguerite Ross Barnett, initiated Partnership for Progress, a collaboration between the

FACING PAGE: Built in 1927, the Ann Whitney Olin Women's Building is actually one of the more recent structures on the Washington University campus. Most of the buildings were constructed in 1904, when both the World's Fair and the Olympic Games used the campus for their events. Photo by James Blank

BELOW: The University of Missouri at St. Louis provides solid preparation in various fields, via its eight academic "schools": arts and sciences, business administration, education, nursing, optometry, graduate studies, night school, and continuing education. Photo by Charles E. Schmidt/Unicorn Stock Photo

community and the university. The project, which emphasizes math and science training, is supported today by many major corporations in the area.

Smaller private institutions that provide quality education in the area include Webster University, Maryville College, Fontbonne College, and Lindenwood College. Webster offers several degrees in the visual and performing arts that draw students from throughout the world.

The *St. Louis Post-Dispatch*, founded by the audacious Joseph Pulitzer in 1880, is known throughout the world today for its investigative reporting and evenhanded coverage of sensitive issues. With the demise of the *Globe-Democrat* in 1986, St. Louis became a one-daily town. This was changed in September 1989 with the appearance of the *St. Louis Sun*, an Ingersoll newspaper, which then folded after only seven months of publication.

The Ingersoll chain has long been active in the St. Louis region with the publication of several editions of

RIGHT AND BELOW: St. Louis' local television stations put the spotlight on community issues and involvement. KPLR-TV is the strongest of the independents, while KETC is the local PBS affiliate. Photo by Charles E. Schmidt/ Unicorn Stock Photo

FACING PAGE: St. Louis' medical community represents an extensive umbrella of expertise available to serve the needs of growing families. Photo by David Burjoski/ HMS Group, Inc.

the *Journal* newspapers. The Journals—Southside, Northside, West County, and so forth—carry neighborhood news and appear twice a week. They are free and therefore count heavily on advertising revenue. A dozen or more other free neighborhood papers, such as the *Westend Word* and the *Webster-Kirkwood Times*, give residents a local slant on "who, what, where, and when."

A popular newspaper with a wide circulation in the area is the weekly *Riverfront Times*, which highlights entertainment in the area as well as providing investigative reporting and a bit of iconoclasm. Papers aimed for a special readership include the *Jewish Light*, the Catholic *St. Louis Review*, and the *Labor Tribune*. The black press is represented by the *St. Louis American*, the *St. Louis*

Argus, and *The Sentinel*. Overseeing both the print and electronic media is the *St. Louis Journalism Review*, which each month analyzes their effectiveness and fairness.

Radio station KMOX, calling itself "the voice of St. Louis," has been intimately connected with the city for 60 years. With a 21.3-percent audience share of the market, KMOX leads the other 40 stations in the area by a wide margin. Its greatest attraction is probably the play-by-play broadcasts of the Cardinals' baseball games, which are heard throughout the Midwest during the summer months. Other popular programs, such as "At Your Service," and call-in talk shows draw thousands of listeners.

Next in line, with a 10-percent market share, is KSHE, an album-oriented rock station that "grew up with St. Louis." It is followed by the usual collection of hard rock, soft rock, top 40, country-western, and oldies stations. Two classical stations, KFUO and National Public Radio's KWMU, which is located on the UMSL campus, offer alternative programming.

Ninety-six percent of all St. Louisans listen to the radio weekly, and they listen an average of more than three hours per day. About $60 million per year is now invested in radio advertising. "Radio is very competitive," says Merrell Hansen, general manager of KSD-FM and KUSA. "There are lots of us in St. Louis and every day you have to work to be better than you were the day before. It's invigorating."

There are eight local television stations in the area. The three network stations have the lion's share of the market, which consists of some 1.1 million television households. William Bolster, director of Multimedia Broadcasting and general manager of the city's leading station, KSDK-TV, says, "The most important element at KSDK is news . . . If I do my job right in making people aware of important issues, they're better informed. I think that television has a responsibility to get people out to vote, to tell people what's going on in their own city."

KETC, the PBS affiliate, also feels a strong responsibility to the city and produces several weekly programs relating to St. Louis' cultural life and civic issues. The strongest independent station is KPLR-TV, which has a 13-percent share of the viewing audience, primarily because it broadcasts Cardinals baseball games. Edward J. Koplar, the station's chief executive officer, sees more growth ahead. "In the next few years we are going to try to localize as much as possible. What we're driving for is that community involvement. We want to concentrate on the type of programming that's going to put the signature on this television station."

As is true in the media everywhere, personalities play an important role in interpreting the city—whether as a newspaper columnist, television anchor, or radio deejay. Some St. Louis media personalities have become minor legends and never fail to draw a crowd when making a personal appearance. "St. Louis is a very personality-oriented market," stresses Hansen.

St. Louis is a major medical center, with almost 80,000 people employed in the health-care industry. The metropolitan area has 56 hospitals, including two teaching medical centers. And apparently, the city is a healthy place to live.

Studies indicate that the health of St. Louisans is comparable to or slightly better than the national average. The number of school and workdays missed is significantly lower in St. Louis than the national average, according to the National Center for Health Statistics.

The ratio of hospital beds to population is above the national average, leading some critics to label the city as "overbedded." This condition has resulted in competition among hospitals for patients and a consequent increase in the number of innovative programs offered. Most large hospitals in the area offer wellness programs that emphasize good nutrition, adequate exercise, and the reduction of stress through psychological health.

Many also have stress units—units aimed at the hard-drinking, hard-driving executive. St. Anthony Hospital's Hyland Center has the largest alcohol/drug rehabilitation program in the area, and in its accommodations is comparable to a fine hotel. The Edgewood Program at St. John's Mercy Medical Center and the independent Care Unit have also been rated highly effective.

Outpatient care, including surgery, is routine at most hospitals. Home health service and occupational medicine are being developed as outreach programs at several institutions.

Both university medical centers have extensive organ transplant programs involving recipients and do-

ABOVE: Barnes Hospital at the Washington University Medical Center attracts patients from around the world for state-of-the-art organ transplant surgeries. Photo by Doug McKay/ HMS Group, Inc.

FACING PAGE, TOP: Dr. Marlene Maxwell examines 8-month-old Kristan Miller at the Salvation Army Clinic. The doctor volunteers her time for routine examinations at the clinic. Photo by Wes Paz

FACING PAGE, BOTTOM: St. Louis' Jewish Hospital contributes several areas of excellence to the region's health-care mix. Photo by Charles E. Schmidt/ Unicorn Stock Photo

nors found throughout the world. Barnes has successfully pioneered heart and lung transplants, while Saint Louis University Medical Center is known for its kidney transplants and renal reconstructive surgery.

St. Louis Children's Hospital, in the Washington University Medical Center, offers specialized care for infants to teenagers. Its neonatal intensive care unit is widely acknowledged as one the best in the nation for pulmonary care.

"St. Louis Children's Hospital was founded out of concern for the health of our region's young people," says Alan W. Brass, the hospital's president. "Underlying our efforts is our belief that all children and adolescents who are sick or injured need to be treated in a children's hospital specializing in their care and needs."

Cardinal Glennon Hospital, part of the Saint Louis University hospital complex, is also for children and is well-known for its trauma unit.

While it is still possible to find a small general hospital in the area, most of the large hospitals are developing specialties. For instance, Jewish Hospital is especially known for its oncology unit, Missouri Baptist Hospital for joint replacements and orthopedic surgery, DePaul for its cardiac and psychiatric units, and St. John's Mercy Medical Center for its obstetrics center. The Mallinckrodt Institute of Radiology is in the forefront of high-tech diagnosis and treatment of a number of diseases. There are a few hospices in the area as well.

St. Louis Regional Hospital, which accepts indigent patients, was recently formed through a merger between the city and county health facilities, both of which have closed.

Cooperation among hospitals seems to be a trend for the 1990s. Rich Van Bokkelen, chief executive officer of Christian Hospital says, "I see hospitals in St. Louis merging . . . There will be the formation of multihospital, noncompetitive alliances, especially among teaching hospitals and hospitals of the same religious affiliations. Hospitals will be able to stay open by complementing each other in noncompeting areas."

In St. Louis city there are 673 physicians per 100,000 residents (the national average is 173 per 100,000) and the great majority are specialists. Most are based at either Barnes or Saint Louis University hospitals in addition to having privileges at other hospitals. Physicians in the county are usually congregated near the large hospitals there.

Although government agencies exist on all levels for the needy, St. Louisans like to take care of their own disadvantaged and do it through a wide variety of social service organizations; some 865 not-for-profit agencies are located in the region. Both service and advocacy organizations look after the needs of children and adults. The major annual drives of the St. Louis Archdiocese, Jewish Federation, Salvation Army, and United Way allocate more than $28 million for human services.

Volunteerism is a definite part of life in St. Louis— art museum docents, zoo friends, gray ladies, literacy tutors, drivers for Meals on Wheels, basketball coaches—the list is endless. Most volunteers report hav-

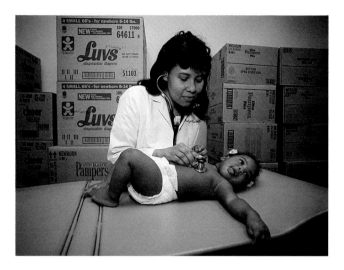

ing fun while they give back to the community a measure of what they feel has been given to them.

Because the scope of human services is so large, several umbrella groups have been formed to provide a coordinated network of organizations for the most needy. Among the larger coalitions are: Community in Partnership, a coalition of 12 human service agencies for homeless families in St. Louis County; Operation Weather Survival, a coalition of service organizations that provide help during extreme hot and cold weather conditions; St. Louis Housing Council, a coalition of emergency shelters and groups supporting low-income housing; Interfaith Partnership, a network of individuals and religious organizations working to meet the survival needs of those living below the poverty line; Household Goods Network, a coalition of agencies that assist homeless families with the basics for housekeeping; Fostercare Coalition, nine agencies that recruit foster parents for children who have been abused, neglected, or abandoned; Health Care for the Homeless Coalition; and Advisory Committee for the Chronically Mentally Ill.

The YMCA and YWCA are strong organizations in the area, offering a multitude of programs. The Boys' Club and Girls' Club are also vigorous, as are a myriad of similar church organizations. Support groups and programs for women in transition can be found in almost every community. Senior Citizens Centers thrive. An outstanding program for seniors is OASIS (Older Americans Information Services), which offers creative programs covering hundreds of topics throughout the city.

CHAPTER SEVEN

Quality of Life

"Music heard so deeply/That is not heard at all, but you are the music/While the music lasts."

—T.S. Eliot
"The Dry Salvages"

Newcomers and old-timers agree—it is "quality of life" that is St. Louis' strongest drawing card. That phrase encompasses both high culture and popular culture, and really means how interesting and fun it is to live in a city.

St. Louis' attractions are affordable and accessible—not all cities can make that claim. From a day at Six Flags over Mid-America to an evening at a dinner theater, entertainment is nearby and tickets are easily available.

Support for the arts comes primarily from individual patrons and from corporate sponsors. Several organized funds, also receiving corporate contributions, underwrite specific productions, such as the Arts and Education Fund and the Mid-America Arts Alliance. City and county residents have voted to tax themselves 24 cents per $100 assessed valuation to support the Art Museum, Missouri Botanical Garden, Science Museum, Zoo, and History Museum. Admission to most of these

These two young men are on their way to a game of basketball along 18th Street in north St. Louis. Photo by Wes Paz

institutions is free, at least part of the time.

The city's greatest source of cultural pride is the St. Louis Symphony Orchestra. No other symphony orchestra in the nation has such heavy corporate backing. Founded in 1845, it is the second oldest orchestra in the nation. Now under the leadership of Leonard Slatkin, the orchestra has found an enthusiastic and loyal audience. Slatkin has installed a chorus, which today is ranked as one of the finest in the country.

The orchestra also is highly regarded by music critics. It was recently rated by *Time* magazine as one of the two best symphony orchestras in the nation and has found worldwide acclaim through its extensive tours. Winner of two Grammy awards and one Emmy, the orchestra's concerts are broadcast weekly on National Public Radio. Symphony concerts are held in Midtown at the elegantly restored Powell Hall, which is said by sound engineers to be almost acoustically perfect.

St. Louis Symphony Orchestra Pops concerts, usually conducted by Richard Hayman, are held every summer at Queeny Park. The tremendously successful concerts feature jazz, old favorites, show tunes, and contemporary popular music.

The St. Louis Conservatory and Schools for the Arts (CASA) encourages talent in the performing arts by offering rigorous training in voice and instrumental music. Well-known international artists perform in concert at CASA each year.

The art of the dance has seen a recent nationwide renaissance, and St. Louis audiences respond to local productions with great enthusiasm. Dance St. Louis is a nonprofit booking group that brings major dance groups to the city. The local dance company, Madco (Mid-America Dance Company), spends much of its time on tour.

Katherine Dunham, a pioneer in modern dance, is a national treasure. Throughout the 1920s and 1930s she studied and choreographed dances based on African and Caribbean folk culture. Several years ago she moved from New York City to East St. Louis, where she established a museum and a popular dance workshop. In a recent *National Geographic* interview based on the book *I Dream a World,* Dunham said, "It was in me to dance, and I had to do it to be satisfied. . . Our production portrayed a part of black people that had not been seen on the stage or in theater." The Katherine Dunham Dancers today perform throughout the world.

St. Louis is a visually exciting city. As Patricia Rice writes in *St. Louis Currents,* "From Louis Sullivan's Wainwright Building to the stenciled gilt art nouveau designs of Union Station's Grand Hall to the sleek lines of West County's St. Louis Priory, the region is marked with national architectural treasure." Landmarks Association was formed in the era of highway building to preserve these treasures. It has several "saves" to its credit today, including the historic DeMenil mansion on the near South Side.

The St. Louis Art Museum in Forest Park is housed in the only exhibition building remaining from the 1904 World's Fair. It was designed by the famed Cass Gilbert (as was the St. Louis Public Library building downtown) and was the first municipally supported art museum in the nation. Among its collections—ranging from ancient to contemporary—its German Expressionist collection is well known. The museum also has one of the most comprehensive and distinguished collections of pre-Columbian art in the nation. Exciting special exhibits draw thousands of visitors each year, and the extensive education program offers classes, workshops, lectures, and a distinguished film series.

Laumeier Sculpture Park presents a unique setting

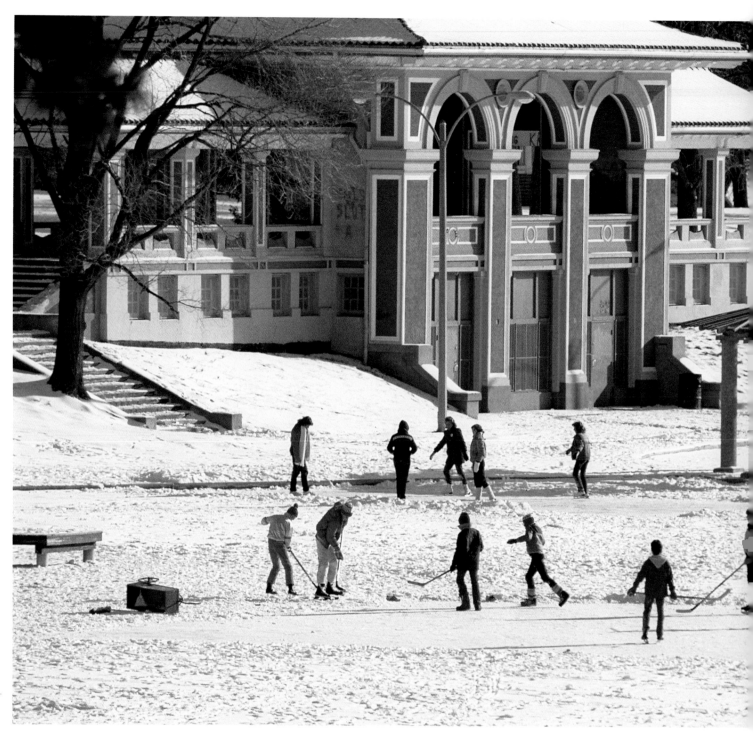

for art—an outdoor exhibition hall. Its focus is on pre-serving monumental sculpture, and it is noted for its collection of pieces by Ernest Trova, a world-renowned sculptor who lives in St. Louis. The permanent collection is imaginatively scattered on lawns and woods throughout the park's 96 acres. The gallery at the park is devoted to modern art, from painting to ceramics, and five new exhibits are mounted each year.

Dozens of small galleries in West County and the Central West End exhibit traditional, contemporary, and avant-garde work, including photography and sculpture. Cupples House at Saint Louis University is a

nineteenth-century mansion designed in the Richard-son Romanesque style. It has been magnificently re-stored and many of its 42 beautifully furnished rooms are now open to the public. An art museum, with changing exhibits, is located in the basement. Much of the permanent collection is religious art. Steinberg Gallery at Washington University has outstanding ex-hibits of contemporary art.

A favorite place for creative people to congregate is the Craft Alliance in University City. The alliance is an organization of visual artists who work in clay, metal, paper, fiber, and glass. Their work—often strikingly

LEFT: Local residents play hockey at Carondelet Park. Photo by Gary Bohn

ABOVE: The Muny, one of the first open-air theatres in America, has been going strong since 1917. Photo by Doug Adams

innovative—is offered for sale at the gallery. Dozens of classes held each year teach the arts of calligraphy, papermaking, weaving, basketry, photography, and ceramics.

Theater is the joy of many St. Louisans. The Repertory Theatre of St. Louis at the Loretto-Hilton Center mixes classics with American standards and innovative drama, and usually offers six impressively staged plays per year. A smaller stage on the lower level introduces contemporary and experimental drama in a more intimate atmosphere.

The Black Repertory Theatre, under director-founder Ron Himes, presents plays written about the black experience. City Players give audiences a chance to see obscure plays and regularly offers world premieres of local residents' work. The Theatre Factory of St. Louis, the Theatre Project Company, and The New Theater (TNT) give local aspiring actors a chance to perform.

Opera Theatre of St. Louis, founded in 1976 by Richard Gaddes at Webster University, has found both critical and popular success with world premieres of commissioned operas, rarely performed operas, and standard repertory operas. Its season is a short one, but heavily attended.

The Muny (once called the Municipal Opera) has been a St. Louis tradition since 1917. On its large outdoor stage it presents big-name stars in such American classic musicals as *The King and I, Camelot,* and *Annie.* One of the first open-air theaters in America, the Muny is synonymous with summer in St. Louis.

The renovated Fox Theater, a 4000-seat Byzantine palace, and the Edison Theater on the Washington University campus book touring companies. One of the most elegant movie theaters in the nation during the 1930s and 1940s, the Fox was restored in the early 1980s under the supervision of Mary Strauss. "Now," says a fan, "it is part Hollywood fantasy, part Indonesian art— all parts gilded." At modest prices, Westport Playhouse in west St. Louis County draws big names, particularly in pop music, comedy, and television. Those who have appeared there in the past include Ben Vereen, The Second City, George Carlin, and Phyllis Diller.

ABOVE: A dinosaur on a leash? Actually, that's just how the Museum of Science and Natural History moves its models around. Photo by Gary Bohn

FACING PAGE: Young St. Louisans "do the Time Warp" one last time at the Varsity Theatre's final showing of the *Rocky Horror Picture Show*. Photo by Wes Paz

St. Louis has a colorful history, which has been carefully preserved so that it can be enjoyed today. A number of historic sites are downtown, beginning with the Gateway Arch and the Museum of Westward Expansion beneath it, which commemorate the westward journey of Lewis and Clark and the settlement of the Western frontier.

The Old Courthouse, across from the Arch, was built in the 1840s in Greek Revival style. The courtroom inside has been restored to the time of the momentous *Dred Scott* decision before the Civil War. Along the riverfront is that engineering marvel of 1874, the Eads Bridge. On the southwest corner of the Arch grounds is the Greek Revival Old Cathedral, now a basilica, which was consecrated in 1834 and was beautifully restored in the 1960s.

Several historic homes in the downtown area have been preserved and are open to the public. Near Defiance, Missouri, 35 miles west of St. Louis, is the Daniel Boone Home, where America's most famous pioneer lived in the early 1800s.

The History Museum in Forest Park, operated by the Missouri Historical Society, carefully documents the cultural changes in the region through dioramas, videos, and other attention-getting displays. The museum is noteworthy for its collection of Indian artifacts (only a fraction of which are displayed), memorabilia relating to black history, and its Charles Lindbergh collection. The Society's educational programs for children and adults have received much acclaim.

A great source of pride for the city is the Missouri Botanical Garden, founded by Henry Shaw in 1859. It has become a botany lab for the world. Director Dr. Peter Raven is a world-renowned botanical expert with extensive experience in Central America and the Andes and who has a deep interest in tropical rain forests. To teach Americans about the fragile ecosystems in these areas, the Garden offers a variety of programs for children and adults. More down-to-earth programs provide how-to information on gardening and raising indoor plants.

The Garden's Climatron is a unique, climate-controlled tropical forest beneath an award-winning geodesic dome which was recently renovated. The exquisite Japanese garden, *Seiwa-En*, the Lehmann rose garden, the English woodland garden, and the herb garden give visitors a rare opportunity to appreciate unusual plants. An annual Japanese Festival held over Labor Day weekend features traditional Japanese art forms: kabuki theater, the tea ceremony ritual, and ikebana (flower arranging). The Garden also operates an arboretum west of the city.

Many parks dot the urban landscape. Tower Grove Park in Midtown was once the estate of Henry Shaw. Forest Park, home of the 1904 World's Fair, is second in size only to New York's Central Park. Its greenhouse, called the Jewel Box, is frequently the scene of weddings and other family celebrations and was the centerpiece for Tennessee Williams' *The Glass Menagerie*.

Also in Forest Park is the St. Louis Zoo, which received national attention through its former director, Marlin Perkins, who hosted the television program "Wild Kingdom" for decades. The zoo's new educational center, the Living World, is a high-tech museum which explains ecology with pizzazz. The zoo also is home to the Jungle of the Apes, a re-created jungle habitat under a large dome housing gorillas, chimps, and orangutans; and Big Cat Country, which allows lions, tigers, cheetahs, and other large felines to roam in an open-air environment.

Nearby in Forest Park is the St. Louis Science Center, which is made up of McDonnell Planetarium and the Monsanto Science Park. It offers playground-type exhibits that demonstrate scientific principles. At the McDonnell Douglas world headquarters, adjacent to the airport, 60 years of aviation history are represented through scale models, dioramas, and pictures.

A unique museum, and one that delights kids of all ages, is the Magic House in Kirkwood. One of the first hands-on museums in the nation, it is a place where visitors "see, touch, explore, and enjoy" the world of science. From the electrostatically charged ball that makes hair fly on end to a three-story spiral slide to talking computers and robots, the Magic House demonstrates that learning is fun.

St. Louis' newest museum is the Dog Museum, located in Queeny Park in West County and housing painting, prints, and sculpture relating to dogs, particularly guide and hunting dogs.

The National Museum of Transport, also in West County, boasts an enormous collection of transporta-

tion vehicles on 50 acres. Civil War-era railroad steam engines, streamlined diesels, vintage automobiles, streetcars, carriages, and historic aircraft all tell the story of America on the move.

Across the Mississippi River in Illinois, the Cahokia Mounds State Historic Site preserves the remains of the largest pre-Columbian city north of Mexico. At Woodhenge, a configuration similar to Stonehenge, the changing of the seasons, including the summer solstice and the spring equinox, is celebrated in early-morning ceremonies.

Since William Marion Reedy initiated *The Mirror* at the turn of the century, there has been an interest in literature in St. Louis. One of the city's best-known authors is Kate Chopin, whose *The Awakening* caused a scandal in 1899. It has recently been reprinted and has become an important part of women's literature. Another well-known St. Louisan is Fannie Hurst, one of the nation's highest paid writers in the 1940s. Her *Imitation of Life* has had three incarnations as a motion picture.

Eugene Field, T.S. Eliot, William Burroughs, Tennessee Williams, and William Inge all lived in St. Louis for a while. Eliot's grandfather, a Unitarian minister, established Washington University. Ntozake Shange, author of the acclaimed *For Colored Girls Who Have Considered Suicide When the Rainbow is Enuf,* lived in the city as a child and recorded her impressions of the critical year 1954 in *Betsy Brown.*

Today, the big literary names in town are William Gass, Howard Nemerov, and Stanley Elkin, who are part of the noted writers' program at Washington University. Novelist David Carkeet teaches at UMSL. Dozens of superb poets call St. Louis home, among them Mona Van Duyn, Constance Urdang, and Donald Finkle. Both poets and novelists are invited to read from their works at evening soirees—the River Styx series at Duff's in the Central West End is the most popular

such event.

Local bookstores and libraries proudly support hometown authors with receptions and book signings. With a total of nearly 5 million items in its various collections, the St. Louis Public Library is an extraordinarily rich resource for the entire community. It maintains comprehensive collections in genealogy, maps, and St. Louis history. Another outstanding source for St. Louis memorabilia and literary history is the private Mercantile Library, the first library established west of the Mississippi River.

In the world of sports, St. Louis is a baseball town. Every other sport has had to compete for whatever time and interest is left over. At one time the city had two teams—the American League Browns and the National League Cardinals. In 1944 they played each other in the World Series, dubbed the "streetcar series," and the city suffered an epidemic of baseball fever that all but closed it down.

The combination of baseball and brewery made it easy to find support for a new stadium. The civic elite rallied to form the Civic Center Redevelopment Corporation, which led to the building of Busch Stadium in 1965. The feeling St. Louisans have for the Cardinals has been compared to that of Brooklynites for the old

Dodgers. It is definitely a hometown team. And because of the scope of the Cardinals radio network, hundreds of thousands of people throughout much of America feel a special affinity toward the Redbirds.

The Cardinals of the National Football League were in St. Louis from 1960 to 1987, when they moved to Phoenix. They won two divisional championships in 1974 and 1975, but were always a poor second to the baseball Cardinals in their number of fans.

A basketball franchise, the St. Louis Hawks, arrived in 1955, and left in 1963. The Spirits, an ABA team, were here for an even briefer period. A professional soccer team, the St. Louis Steamers, came, left, and was succeeded by the St. Louis Storm during the 1980s.

The Blues hockey team plays at the Arena. In the past few years, the image of the Blues has changed from that of a rough, brawling team to that of a competitive team that provides exhilarating family entertainment. Blues season ticket sales have skyrocketed. Blues management, copying techniques used successfully by the Cardinals, offers senior citizen night, high school night, and college night, with special prices for the targeted groups.

College sports are not a big draw in the area, except for the Saint Louis University basketball team, the Billik-

ins, which finished second in the National Invitational Tournament in 1989 and 1990. Fans in the region also support the teams of the University of Missouri and the University of Illinois.

St. Louis has a notable tradition in two other sports. Dwight Davis, the donor of the Davis Cup, helped establish tennis in the region, and the name of the Forest Park courts commemorates his role. St. Louis was at one time the bowling capital of the country. Budweiser and Falstaff sponsored teams that dominated the sport and produced such greats as Dick Weber, Don Carter, Laverne Carter, and Billy Welu.

Fittingly, when the American Bowling Congress built its Hall of Fame, it chose St. Louis as the site. In the museum, the history of bowling—from ancient Egypt to the present—is imaginatively exhibited, with videodiscs, visitor-activated computers, and functioning old-time bowling alleys. At the St. Louis Sports Hall of Fame at Busch Stadium, the emphasis is on baseball, football, basketball, and hockey.

Several St. Louis athletes have become stars through the Olympics, such as boxers Leon and Michael Spinks and track superstar Jackie Joyner-Kersee. St. Louis was the home of the first Olympic games played in the United States—at the 1904 World's Fair—

Baseball fans, many of them loyally garbed in Cardinal red, pack Busch Stadium for the city's most adored sport. Photo by James Blank

and it became the home of the first Senior Olympics in 1988.

Along the riverfront, the excursion boats *Huck Finn, Becky Thatcher,* and *The President* offer delightful cruises on the Mississippi. The riverboat *Robert E. Lee* is a very fine restaurant.

Just north of the Arch, Laclede's Landing, a former warehouse district of nine blocks, has been restored as a nineteenth-century neighborhood of cobblestone streets and wrought-iron streetlamps. It has become a popular entertainment center, where good food, drink, and music can be found on every corner.

The restored Union Station downtown has become a fashionable amusement center with dozens of restaurants, shops, movie theaters, and live entertainment.

Southwest of the city is Grant's Farm, where President Ulysses S. Grant once lived and farmed. It is a picturesque 281-acre game preserve owned by Anheuser-Busch and filled with wild (and tame) animals. Visitors tour the area by tram with a stop at the stables of the famous Clydesdales.

At Six Flags Over Mid-America, west of St. Louis near Eureka, the region's history is celebrated with amusement-park rides and live entertainment. No one claims that the history portrayed there is accurate, but it is exciting and fun. Its multiloop roller coaster roars at 65 mph through loops, spirals, and a double corkscrew.

In recent years the St. Louis VP (for Veiled Prophet)

Fair has become known throughout the nation. Over 100 years ago, on October 8, 1878, the mysterious Veiled Prophet of Khorassan made his first visit to the city. After he arrived by barge he led an elaborate procession through the downtown streets. Torchbearers preceded him and fireworks followed him to the Merchant's Exchange building, which had been temporarily transformed into the "Temple of Ceres." The appearance of the prophet—whose identity has never been revealed—signaled the opening of the social season, later evolving into the formal presentation of debutantes at the VP Ball.

While the Veiled Prophet Ball was reserved for the city's elite, the parade preceding the ball was always a time for citywide celebration. During the 1960s, when there was agitation for the democratization of many institutions, the VP celebration lost much support because of its white, Anglo-Saxon, and Protestant flavor. Since then the celebration has been moved from October to the Fourth of July weekend, and the invitation to attend has been extended to the whole world.

Now the VP Fair is billed as "the nation's biggest birthday party" and is held along the riverfront for four days of food, balloon races, music—often several name bands are performing at the same time on the various stages set up in the area—riverboat races, air shows, and dancing. Each night ends with spectacular fireworks.

In June ragtimers from around the country gather to pay tribute to St. Louis' Scott Joplin at the National Ragtime Festival on the riverfront. Some 40 entertainers perform each night for a week. Joplin's home on Delmar Boulevard has been slated for restoration into a national museum of ragtime.

St. Louis likes to celebrate its German heritage. In outlying towns the fall Oktoberfest and spring Maifest regularly draw crowds. In late July the Strassenfest is held in the city each year, turning the streets into a huge polka party. There's always plenty of food, brew, dancing, and authentic German oompah-pah bands.

Other neighborhood celebrations—whether ethnic, artsy-craftsy, or geographical—occur periodically. One

LEFT: St. Louisan Mike Seebold takes a victory lap after winning the Bud Light World Championship Grand Prix Boat Races at George Winter Park in Fenton. Photo by Wes Paz

FACING PAGE: The nearby Six Flags Over Mid-America offers fun with a historical flavor—and also some state-of-the-art thrills. Photo by Terry Barner/ Unicorn Stock Photo

BELOW: Enough is enough! After all the excitement and action, there's a lot to be said for a peaceful place like Carondelet Park, and some quiet, quality time with a friend. Photo by Gary Bohn

of the best is the Jour de Fete, held in Ste. Genevieve each August. Another is the St. Charles Riverfest, held over the Fourth of July holidays, or the Festival of the Little Hills, held in August. St. Charles, only 30 minutes west of St. Louis, is the oldest city on the Missouri River and was the starting point for the Lewis and Clark expedition.

CHAPTER EIGHT

The View from the Top

"The fortunes of the inhabitants of this city may fluctuate, you and I may sink into oblivion and our families become extinct, but the progress of our city is morally certain; the causes of its prosperity are inscribed upon the very face of the earth, and are as permanent as the foundations of the soil and the sources of the Mississippi."

—*William Carr Lane,*
First Mayor of St. Louis, 1823

S t. Louis leadership is based firmly in the business community. Although elected government officials play an important role in steering the city and in determining its future, they could not do so without the backing of business and industry.

"The single most significant source of leadership in the St. Louis region comes from the corporate chief executive officers of the major locally headquartered firms," states E. Terrence Jones in *St. Louis Currents.* "Not only do these individuals command

Seen from the top of the Arch, St. Louis appears as an industrial and financial leader in today's fast-moving business environment. Photo by Bill McMackins/ Unicorn Stock Photo

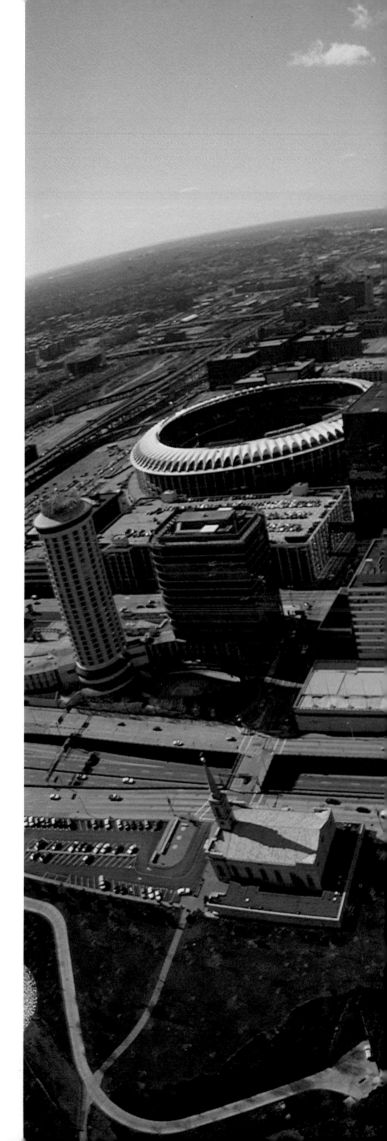

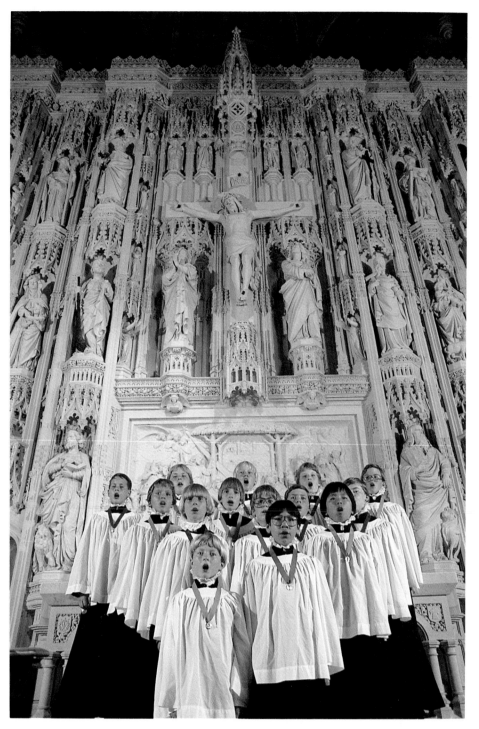

ABOVE: The St. Louis Boys Choir sings before the altar at the Christ Church Cathedral. Photo by Odell Mitchell, Jr.

FACING PAGE: St. Louis' dedicated citizens make the city one of the most livable in the nation. Photo by Gary Bohn

the resources of huge national and multinational organizations, but they also coordinate their power by working through Civic Progress."

Civic Progress, an organization made up of about two dozen chief executive officers, was organized in the late 1950s to oversee passage of an important bond issue. Since then the group has become largely effective in securing voter approval for major public or quasipublic capital projects and in fund-raising for both cultural and social welfare activities. Currently Civic Progress is supporting the expansion of Cervantes Convention Center, the effort to bring a professional football team to St. Louis, and increased assistance to area public schools.

But it does not set the community's agenda for action—that generally comes from the mayor's office, from the initiative of elected officials, or from citizens with a deep interest in a particular issue.

For instance, most environmental improvement projects, from planting flowers on boulevards to making sure that clean-air standards are met, result from the continued action of strong citizens groups in concert with the media. Garden clubs and political activists alike want to keep St. Louis a healthy, attractive place to live.

To honor outstanding community leaders, the Man of the Year Award was begun by the *St. Louis Globe-Democrat* in 1955. Today, because the *Globe-Democrat* has disappeared from the city, the *Post-Dispatch* cooperates in its presentation. The award is presented annually to the person who "best exemplifies an inspiring level of civic and industrial leadership to generate a spirit of conviction, purpose and confidence in the development of the greater St. Louis area."

The men chosen for these awards have shaped the destiny of the city. In recent years Charles Knight, chief executive officer of Emerson Electric, Lee Liberman of Laclede Gas Company, and Robert Hyland of CBS/KMOX radio were selected.

In 1987 the award went to August Busch III,

chairman of the board and president of Anheuser-Busch Companies. In accepting it he said, "St. Louis is a model of what an American city can be. The basically cooperative relationship of the city and the county, the support and involvement of the business community, the ongoing participation of strong community and neighborhood organizations, and the ongoing quality of active news media all contribute to the resurgent health of our metropolitan area."

white and male, more women and blacks are being heard than ever before. Harriet Woods, recently Missouri's lieutenant governor, began her political career on the University City board. Other outstanding women include legislators Sheila Lumpe and Sue Shear, County Council member Ellen Conant, and Marguerite Ross Barnett, chancellor of the University of Missouri-St. Louis.

Opportunities for leadership by women are found

Two important organizations also provide leadership for the region. The East-West Gateway Coordinating Council was founded in 1965 as an association of governments in Missouri and Illinois. The council plans developments in transportation, environment, land use, and metropolitan development.

The Regional Commerce and Growth Association (RCGA) began in 1836 as an organization of businessmen with an interest in strengthening the economy of the area. Today the majority of businesses in the region support the organization (formerly the Chamber of Commerce) with their money, time, and enthusiasm. A full range of activities allows for leaders to emerge on all levels.

Although the most effective leadership in the city is

in the Junior League, League of Women Voters, National Council of Jewish Women, and YWCA, among dozens of other organizations. The YWCA presents Women of the Year awards annually. The Urban League and the NAACP, the latter directed by long-time civil rights advocate Ina Boon, offer blacks a strong voice in the region. Boon sees the role of blacks as one of constantly striving for justice. With the increase of the number of blacks active in politics in the last 20 years, justice is closer than ever to reality.

The popularity of St. Louis Mayor Vincent Schoemehl has been attributed not only to his personableness, but also his capacity for hard work and his determination to keep St. Louis one of the most liveable cities in the nation. His "Operation Brightside" has

FACING PAGE: A frequent stop for visitors to St. Louis is the futuristic Climatron at the Missouri Botanical Gardens. Tourism remains a strong industry for the region. Photo by James Blank

BELOW: Radio-controlled boats set a peaceful pace during the Sailboat Regatta at Tilles Park. Photo by Gary Bohn

each year to participate in a yearlong program to enhance their own skills and to develop a network of informed people who will guide the direction of change in our community, according to Carolyn Losos, director of the organization.

As St. Louis leaders look to the future, they see the 1990s as exciting and challenging. A few predictions about the growth of the region can be made.

Without question, smokestack industries will con-

given new heart to city residents and beautified the city as well. Long-time County Executive Gene McNary recently moved to Washington, D.C., as director of the Immigration/Naturalization Administration for the Bush administration. H.C. Milford is his successor.

Representative Dick Gephardt of Missouri's Third Congressional District is recognized as a contender in national politics, and was seriously considered as a presidential candidate in the 1988 election. He is currently majority leader of the U.S. House of Representatives.

Another important leader is Roman Catholic Archbishop John May. He has proved to be an extraordinary asset to the city, both as head of the large St. Louis archdiocese and as head of the American Bishops Conference.

In order to encourage the development of leadership in all segments of society, Leadership St. Louis was founded in 1971. Approximately 50 persons from the private, public, and volunteer sectors are selected

tinue to disappear, to be replaced by "clean" industry, particularly high-tech and biomedical enterprises. The labor force must continue to learn new skills in order to adapt to rapidly changing technologies. Therefore, the region's training schools, colleges, and universities will continue to grow, and the ties between business and education will be strengthened.

The service industries too will expand, especially in the fields of finance and medicine. Several million people in the Midwest are dependent on the St. Louis region for these services. As the city expands as a biotechnical center, more and more small "cottage industries" will find niches to establish new, highly specialized products and services.

As a transportation center, St. Louis will continue to expand. Lambert-St. Louis International Airport recently announced plans to double its size and capacity within the next few years. The light rail system running from East St. Louis through downtown St. Louis to Lambert

will offer an important alternative to automobile traffic.

A very important segment of the region's economy is the convention and tourism business. This segment is growing rapidly and will continue to do so, as Cervantes Convention Center expands and new hotels are built downtown. An aggressive marketing campaign is bringing hundreds of regional and national meetings to the city, and exciting cultural events, outstanding museums, and amusement cen-

ters attract more tourists every year.

Population growth continues westward into St. Charles County and southward into Jefferson County. Business, industry, and the retail trade follow. A modest growth to the east, into Illinois, is also noticeable. As a result of this expansion, there will need to be a stronger emphasis on regional government, especially in law enforcement and the development of transportation systems.

Illinois side is saddled with that state's single most economically depressed city, East St. Louis, which ironically was once second only to Chicago in prosperity. Today that city is surrounded by communities with great promise, but until its social, economic, and political ills are under control, it will continue to depress the entire region and reflect poorly on St. Louis. Despite the best efforts of the East-West Gateway Council and Bi-State Development, no progress has been made toward improving conditions in East St. Louis.

Few cities in the United States have better race relations than St. Louis, yet, much needs to be achieved. Although the black population of the city of St. Louis is currently just under 50 percent, that percentage is not reflected in civic or cultural leadership. True integration—in education, residential patterns, and social interactions—is years away.

St. Louis County is divided into almost 100 communities—a political balkanization detrimental to true metropolitan cohesiveness, but suburban residents doggedly hold on to small-town advantages while deploring the lack of adequate services available in such communities. Growth is inhibited without metropolitan unity, yet the move to consolidate governments seems to threaten the unique identity of each community and is met with stiff opposition.

These problems may seem to be major impediments to the progress of the region, and indeed they could be. Therefore, it is all the more remarkable that St. Louis has not only advanced to a premier position as one of America's most livable communities, but continues to build upon its outstanding quality of life. There is a feeling of pride in St. Louis today—not mere boosterism, but a genuine warmth for the community and commitment to making it better.

As St. Louis approaches the twenty-first century, it has much to offer its residents and its visitors—a low cost of living, a central location, a friendly climate, and exciting attractions. The site that Pierre Laclède and Auguste Chouteau chose for their village has indeed fulfilled its promise.

Although it is not difficult to paint a rosy picture of the future of St. Louis, it would be unrealistic to presume that the future will be without difficulties.

Perhaps the most serious problem is created by the Mississippi River, the geographic feature responsible for the early success of the community. It is now a divisive element, a state line. But it is more—it fragments what should be a cohesive metropolitan entity into two separate enclaves. The Missouri side thrives, but the

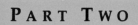

PART TWO

St. Louis' Enterprises

Photo by Odell Mitchell, Jr.

CHAPTER NINE

Manufacturing

Production and distribution of goods and foodstuffs provide employment for many St. Louis area residents.

Photo by Martha McBride/
Unicorn Stock Photos

Nooter Corporation

Quietly nestled on St. Louis' south side, Nooter Corporation continues its dynamic growth as a worldwide custom steel and alloy plate fabricator of heavy processing equipment.

Located on convenient railroad routes and with direct access to the Mississippi River, Nooter custom fabricates a wide variety of pressure vessels, large reactors, heat exchangers, and tanks. Nooter's custom equipment serves the brewing, chemical, cogeneration, food processing, petrochemical, petroleum, pharmaceutical, power, pulp and paper, and space industries.

"Nooter's skilled employees can fabricate and weld all weldable metals," says Ralph V. Streiff, Nooter's chairman of the board. To be able to say that is special because of the wide variety of alloys and pure metals that are available.

Nooter has been building custom process equipment for almost 100 years. Every contract is unique to a customer's specifications. With a fabrication range up to six-inch thick material and a capacity to lift 500 tons, Nooter has assembled a unique array of specialized equipment and is known worldwide as the premier fabricator of reactive metals, such as titanium and zirconium.

John Nooter, an immigrant from Holland, started Nooter Corporation in 1896. Nooter implemented his sail-rigging skills by working for John O'Brien Boiler Works prior to starting his own business. His company's first contract was to paint the trolley poles on the old Lindell Railway Line. From that, Nooter earned enough money to buy a hand punch and a sheet-metal bending roll. Nooter became a stack maker, then a boilermaker, and then pioneered in welding stainless steel and other alloys. In 1949 the company changed its name from John Nooter Boiler Works Company to Nooter Corporation to better describe the direction the company was taking.

About 700 of Nooter's employees belong to AFL-CIO International Brotherhood of Boilermakers, Iron Shipbuilders, Blacksmiths, Forgers,

A new 128-ton regenerator head is lifted into place as part of a multimillion-dollar turnaround by Nooter Construction Company for a Montana refinery.

and Helpers. Nooter Corporation's main plant spans 57 acres with 700,000 square feet under roof.

In the 1950s Nooter Corporation acquired Missouri Boiler and Tank Co., now a division, and established St. Louis Metallizing Co. as a subsidiary. Missouri Boiler originally supplemented the work of the parent organization by fabricating steel and alloy vessels of lighter materials in thicknesses up to 1.5 inches and 50 tons in weight. Now the emphasis is on heat-recovery steam-generating equipment weighing up to 200 tons.

St. Louis Metallizing is one of the largest contract

A 130-foot-long stainless-steel oxidation tower.

ABOVE: This 355,000-pound reactor is
being loaded at Nooter's Mississippi River
dock for shipment to a southern chemical
processor.

RIGHT: Nooter craftspeople install
"flights" in this Hastelloy hydrofluoric-
acid reactor section.

metallizing shops in the country.
The company does not only hard-
surfacing by such methods as oxy-
acetylene and shielded arc, but it
also rebuilds and protects worn
parts by thermal spraying.

Nooter Construction Company, a
subsidiary, provides a full range of
field construction services: new construction, maintenance, and petroleum refinery turnarounds. With
offices in St. Louis and Philadelphia,
this construction company subsidiary combines progressive computerized project scheduling and
management techniques with skilled
field craftsmanship to furnish quality equipment to the petroleum,
chemical, pulp and paper, brewing,

and power industries.

McGrath & Associates, Inc., a
majority-owned subsidiary, serves
as a general contractor, building industrial and commercial buildings.

Nooter Corporation had not made
boilers for more than 40 years until it
acquired Eriksen Engineering Co. in
1987 and formed a wholly owned
subsidiary known as Nooter/Eriksen
Cogeneration Systems, Inc. This subsidiary is a single-source supplier of
boilers and heat-recovery systems

designed to conserve energy from
various sources of heat.

"We have been told that there is
no company in the world quite like
Nooter," Streiff says. "We pride our-
selves especially on our technical involvement in the industry." In this
regard, Nooter is represented by key
people on committees of the American Society of Mechanical Engineers,
the American Society of Metal-
lurgists, and the American Institute
of Chemical Engineers. These organizations set the standards by which
pressure vessels are built to with-
stand the high pressure and tempera-
tures to which they are subjected.

As Nooter provides expertise ex-
ternally, the firm has also advanced
expertise in internal management. It
uses the management and quality
programs of John Nooter, developed
long before similar programs cred-
ited to the Japanese swept the
United States. Nooter himself started
the program whereby employees
share in the ownership of the company. As a result, one-third of
Nooter Corporation's 1,200 employees own stock, some of which had
been bought on the installment plan.
Upon their deaths, their shares are
sold back to the privately held company to perpetuate the program.

"Because employees own a stake
in the company, they also have a say
in its running, which encourages
commitment," says Streiff. Employees sit down monthly with management in round-robin discussions.
Management explains the company's current situation, for example contracts and backlog, and the
employees discuss their needs, even
needs as small as a light bulb that
needs replacing. "The employees,"
says Streiff,"are often the ones who
come up with ways to make production better, faster, easier, and
smarter."

Sunnen Products Co.

Space shuttles would never soar without honing. Ice cream machines would not put the topspin on ice cream without honing. Carpet filaments, laboratory equipment, and glass syringes all depend on honing at some point in their production. Sunnen Products Co. is in the business of honing (finishing) holes, primarily in metal products. The company manufactures 19 standard machines that are kept in stock for immediate shipment. It also, from time to time, builds one-of-a-kind, specialized machines.

BELOW LEFT: The labor-saving Sunnen model 1804 honing machine is considered to be the workhorse of the metalworking industry.

BELOW RIGHT: Sunnen's precision bore-sizing processes are well known throughout the automotive engine rebuilding and industrial metalworking industries for their unique crosshatch pattern—ideal for supporting a uniform film of lubrication.

Sunnen Products makes holes from a 60,000th of an inch to five inches in diameter—with more precision than a line of Rockettes. When Sunnen began in 1927, no honing machine existed; all honing was done with hand tools. Then honing was mostly used to rebuild automobiles. Sunnen introduced abrasives for portable honing tools, which were used in conjunction with hand drills.

Before World War II Sunnen made and sold automotive-oriented products to people who rebuilt engines, but during the war Sunnen concentrated on the industrial market. After the war Sunnen set up an industrial division to sell to other manufacturers. "If we sell a honing machine to Ford Motor Company, that's industrial," explains James K. Berthold, president and chairman. "If we sell a similar product to Mendenhall Rebuilders in downtown St. Louis, that's from

Jim Berthold, president and chairman (left), and the late Bob Sunnen inspect Sunnen's unique CrossGrinding™ machine, which combines computer technology and advanced tooling to create a truly next-generation system.

the automotive aftermarket division." Three-quarters of Sunnen's business is industrial; one-quarter is automotive aftermarket.

Specifically, Sunnen's products fall into four categories: honing machines that use abrasives to size or finish a hole, the tooling those machines use, the abrasives that go with the tooling, and accessories, such as Sunnen's line of gauges. A related but independent category concerns boring machines, which use a different process than honing to finish bores.

In 1986 Sunnen purchased Tobin-Arp Co. in Minnesota and moved it to St. Louis. Tobin-Arp made boring equipment

that resizes an engine cylinder or engine rod by using steel tools rather than abrasives to size the hole.

Sunnen exports all four lines of its products. As an exporter Sunnen is no slouch—the company has been honored with the "E" Star Award, presented ceremoniously by the president of the United States. "There is no place we couldn't or won't export to, but at varying times, protective restrictions won't permit us to export to some countries," says Berthold.

More than 25 percent of Sunnen's total business is from the export trade. Sixty-eight percent of that is exported to Western Europe. In

RIGHT: A state-of-the-art Sunnen research facility is dedicated to the study and technological advancement of bore sizing and finishing.

BELOW: Sunnen's extensive product line is manufactured in a spacious 401,000-square-foot plant equipped with the most modern production equipment and high-quality control systems.

years past the European market was 80 percent of Sunnen's export business, but the Far East has been coming on strong recently, according to William Martinez, a Sunnen director and former international consultant.

As an export agent before he was employed by Sunnen, Martinez started in October 1945 to export to markets in countries "south of the border" (countries not at war). During 1947 and 1948 he exported to neutral Switzerland, and in 1950 he visited Europe, concentrating on countries with Marshall Plan dollars, such as France and Holland. "All the firms I signed on then are still our distributors," says Martinez.

In the early days of exporting, only automotive equipment was considered. "There was a big need for that after the war," Martinez explains. In 1950 some in-

dustrial equipment was exported, principally to places such as Hawaii and Alaska (before they were states) and to Europe.

To compete in the European market, Martinez recognized that Sunnen's industrial distributors needed technical training in order to sell the firm's sophisticated equipment. So he organized his marketing staff to meet with distributors, and together they called on customers to teach them how to sell the equipment. "Distributors were not used to having this service," Martinez recalls.

Sunnen's international policy continues to be one where Sunnen does not run the show, but shows others how. "We hire local people," Berthold says.

Berthold added that Sunnen expects to do more business with the Soviet Union under its current government. "Remi Wrona, our vice president of Sunnen International, was hired to build and maintain and constantly improve our worldwide distribution network," Berthold says. "We have a product that's good—the best in the world. A distributor can make money with this product if everything is done correctly. If he can't, you don't have his loyalty."

Berthold, whose office windows

look out onto busy Manchester Road in Maplewood, a suburb of St. Louis, says the product is backed by service that other companies would shake their heads at. Sunnen has replaced and retrofitted products at no charge. Also, customers can send a product to St. Louis at no charge and have Sunnen test it to determine what costs are entailed.

As a further service, Sunnen makes every attempt to ship domestic orders on the same day they are received. A sophisticated computer system cuts handling time. Sunnen, furthermore, maintains a huge inventory—more than 7,000 different items. "Our goal is that 90 percent of domestic orders are sent out on the same day they're received," states Berthold.

Domestically, Sunnen does not sell to distributors but to end users. In the United States alone, Sunnen has 30,000 active accounts.

Overseas, the company has 70 distributors.

When the nation's businesses are healthy, so is Sunnen's, selling brand-spanking-new equipment; when the country is in an economic recession or depression, Sunnen's business remains solid, springing from repairs and rebuilding. "That helps us cush-

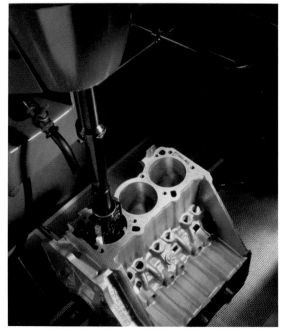

ion our cycles," Berthold explains.

Sunnen continues to make the products it introduced decades ago, such as the basic portable hone in the half-inch electric drill, thousands of which are sold annually, and the cylinder king, a product first manufactured 25 years ago. The cylinder king is the second generation of a machine now in more than 2,500 shops in the automotive engine-rebuilding industry. The cylinder king corrects taper, out-of-round, and other conditions that cause engine blocks to need reconditioning.

LEFT: Sunnen's honing lab is a unique technical facility fully equipped to train Sunnen distributors and representatives in the operation and maintenance of Sunnen's complete product line.

BELOW LEFT: The model CV-616 vertical honing machine puts a precision-honed, new-engine finish on the cylinder walls of engine blocks during the rebuilding process.

BELOW RIGHT: Sunnen's precision bore-sizing gauges are used wherever precision is a must—for in-process inspection, receiving inspection, laboratory analysis, and all facets of automotive engine rebuilding.

RIGHT: Sunnen manufactures and stocks thousands of varieties and sizes of mandrels and stones for virtually any honing application in all types of materials.

BELOW: Diamond tooling for Sunnen's valve and seat guide machine has increased the productivity of automotive machine shops worldwide.

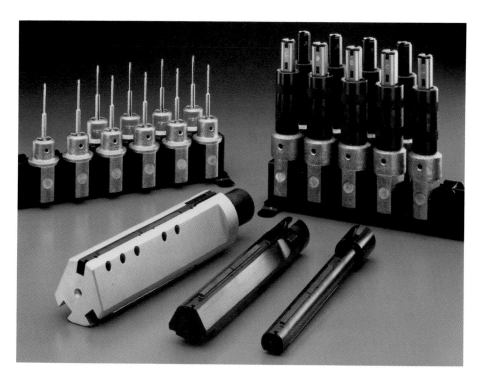

Sunnen makes all kinds of honing stones—aluminum oxide, silicon carbide, diamonds, and cubic boron nitride. Furthermore, Sunnen has a complete research department dedicated to the study and advancement of honing-stone technology.

Historically, nearly all abrasive development has been directed to the grinding process. Radically different operating conditions unique to honing dictate a radically different approach to the formulation of honing stones. Sunnen grades and qualifies every honing stone shipped.

Berthold credits the founder, Joseph Sunnen, with being more than just a mechanical genius. "He established the groundwork for a progressive management style. He took care of his rank and file."

In 1941 Joe Sunnen set up a profit-sharing trust, one of the first in the nation that has paid the full amount under the law in deferred income. Of a more frivolous but equally compassionate nature, Sunnen Products Co. holds a watermelon feast in the park behind the plant. On a hot August day workers welcome the time off. In June a workday is abandoned for the company picnic.

"We treat people as mature adults," says Berthold. "Ninety-five percent live up to the standards, but we don't promulgate rules that affect everybody because of the 5 percent that don't."

The treatment pays off. Attendence at the Sunnen plant stays high at 98 percent. Employees sit on an advisory board and every other month join in a roundtable discussion; three or four times per year officers hold a meeting to bring employees up to date. These methods of management were in place long before they became popular in the 1980s. "We've always managed by the walking around principle," explains Berthold.

Berthold is the first nonmember of the Sunnen family to be president and chairman of the company. Bob Sunnen, son of founder Joe Sunnen, was president from 1973 to 1987 and served as chairman until his death in 1990.

Although there are many ways to finish holes, Berthold does not worry too much about competition. "We are the world's largest company

selling integrated products specifically devoted to honing," says Berthold. "If a company doesn't require an accurate hole, it doesn't need our products. But if accuracy is a factor, no one in the market can beat Sunnen honing as a high-quality, cost-effective method of bore sizing and finishing."

Pet Incorporated

Although Pet Incorporated sometimes receives calls from people looking for pets, almost everyone with a pantry knows the company stands for food, not animals. However, it is a cow that looks out from the label on Pet Evaporated Milk, the product most associated with the St. Louis firm.

Evaporated milk, product of a new process and sold in a revolutionary tin, turned the company into a household name in the late nineteenth century. Now more than 100 years old, Pet Incorporated is a leading producer of packaged convenience foods around the world. Annual sales are more than $1.8 billion per year, $180 million of which comes from international sales.

Pet has 40 plants in 17 states and eight countries. The company is a subsidiary of Whitman Corporation,

a consumer goods and services firm that also owns Midas International, Pepsi-Cola General Bottlers, and Hussmann Corp. Pet employs more than 9,000 people, 500 of whom work in the headquarters overlooking the Mississippi River in downtown St. Louis. The building itself heralds a timeless architecture of no particular era; thus it is as often mistaken for modern as traditional.

The company, which began in a small Illinois dairy town in 1885, continues to grow in three principal ways: from new products or extensions of existing lines, from acquisitions, and from geographic expansion. Domestically, Pet has successfully increased distribution of the Old El Paso products, which originated in the Southwest. Distribution of Progresso products, traditionally strong in the Northeast, is expanding

from coast to coast. Internationally, Pet will expand through new products as well as broader distribution.

One of Pet's most exciting international stories has been the remarkable acceptance and growth of its Old El Paso brand of Mexican foods. Already distributed in more than 30 countries worldwide, the popular line shows signs of becoming one of those rare, truly international brands of widespread renown.

In addition to Old El Paso, Pet manufactures and markets other Mexican foods, such as Las Palmas enchiladas and red cooking sauces and Pancho Villa taco shells, dinners, and sauces.

Pet's Italian food products are sold under the labels of Progresso

A colorful arrangement of a few of Pet's popular food products.

Pet Incorporated's headquarters building overlooks the Mississippi River and the famous Gateway Arch.

(sauces, condiments, oils, and canned soups) and Montini (canned tomatoes).

In the category of meat spreads, beans, and spices, Pet manufactures and markets Underwood (deviled ham and other meat spreads and a variety of canned sardines), B&M (a wide variety of baked beans and brown bread), Accent Flavor Enhancer and Sa-son Accent (seasoning), Friend's (baked beans and brown bread), and Mi Secrito (condiments).

In the line of desserts and breakfast foods, Pet manufactures and sells Pet-Ritz (frozen pie crust shells, fruit and cream pies, seasonal mince and pumpkin pies, and fruit cobblers), Downyflake (frozen breakfast meals, waffles, pancakes, and French toast), Whitman's (frozen layered cream pies), Oronoque (frozen pie crust shells), La Creme (frozen whipped topping), Pet Whip (frozen nondairy whipped topping), Heartland (cereals), and Evans (ice cream toppings and syrups).

Other Pet brands include Dairymate and Sego (liquid diet food), Hain (natural foods such as oils, soups, and condiments), Hollywood (health foods such as specialty vegetable oils, carrot juice, and salad dressings), Van de Kamp's (frozen seafood), Orval Kent (refrigerated salads), and Whitman's (sampler and other candies).

Some of these brands define America's cooking history. The process to evaporate milk was introduced at the turn of the century. Among the most popular brands was Our Pet, sold in "baby-size" cans for a nickel each. Its popularity gave the company, begun as Helvetia Milk Condensing Co., a new name in 1924. In 1955 Pet-Ritz pies became the company's first acquisition outside of its traditional milk business. Then came Downyflake Waffles, which joined the company in 1963, making breakfast foods another good complement to Pet's milk products.

With the acquisition of the Wm. Underwood Co. in 1982, Pet added a meat product with a red devil dancing on the label. The red devil, designed in 1867, is America's oldest registered food trademark in use today. Another Pet product with a famous trademark, the Whitman's Sampler, comes in a box that looks like a sampler of cross stitches and linen-like texture. It contains a candy index on the inside—the first box of candy to aid the "chocoholic" in discovering what filling is inside each chocolate. Sego, another Pet product, was the first liquid diet food geared toward the positive aspects of health—all others at the time were marketed against obesity rather than toward health.

Pet continues to pursue the health food business with its Hain and Hollywood brands, which it acquired along with Progresso in 1986.

At the present time, most of the company's natural and health food products are sold through health food stores. But the trend toward healthier eating is not a fad, according to company officials, and Pet hopes to respond to growing consumer demand by taking the health food business into mainstream supermarkets.

As Pet Incorporated responded to the need for stable milk products at the turn of the last century, it is responding to America's dietary demands for healthier foods at the turn of the next one. A good citizen of St. Louis as well as a progressive manufacturer, Pet looks to the twenty-first century from its vantage in the center of the nation on the Mississippi River, overlooking the grounds of the famous Gateway Arch.

Slay Industries

Slay Industries is a St. Louis-based transportation company that was founded in the 1920s by John R. Slay, a highly-decorated veteran returning from World War I. From its roots as a local trucking firm, the company grew under the leadership of Slay and his son, Eugene, to become a nationally recognized transporter of liquid and dry-bulk products.

Slay Industries' location in the heart of America has played a key role in building the diversified company that provides bulk motor transportation, comprehensive river-port transshipment services, barge fleeting and harbor service, facility construction and maintenance, and full-service warehousing.

According to Keith A. Rhodes, vice president of finance and administration, Slay Industries has come a long way from its days as Slay Drayage. But some things remains the same.

"Quality is a real focus today in American industry," he says. "But Slay has been providing quality service safely to our customers since the very beginning. We are committed to continuous process improvement. Our goal in providing services to our customers is zero deviation or defects. We like to say quality is our driving force."

Slay approaches the zero deviation or defects goal from several angles. First, employees work closely with customers to determine their expectations, then they are committed to delivering on those expectations. Slay facilities and equipment are continually being expanded to meet the growth needs of its customers and to enhance their profitability.

Second, the company recently installed one of the most advanced, computerized systems in the transportation industry. The system makes it possible to monitor ship-

Cahokia Marine Service is a multimodal transportation complex located on the Mississippi River directly across from downtown St. Louis.

ments on line and in real time and to communicate with customers electronically. This translates into better customer service in the form of up-to-the-minute arrival schedules and accurate, timely invoicing.

Customers also benefit from Slay Industries' commitment to safety. The company's safety record is one of the best in the transportation business. Before they are qualified to handle customer products, Slay employees and owner-operators are required to complete rigorous safety training programs. They also receive additional safety training on an ongoing basis.

Slay Industries' far-reaching transportation services touch customers nationwide, and its divisions operate in an increasingly global marketplace. One such division is Slay Transportation, a winner of several National Tank Truck Carriers safety awards. Slay Transportation operates more than 250 specialized trailers and is one of the

most modern fleets in the industry. The company has 48-state common carrier and contract authority, broker authority, and is licensed in portions of Canada. Truck terminals are strategically located throughout the southern, midwestern, and eastern United States.

Another division is Slay Bulk Terminals, a full-service liquid-distribution terminal, certified to store or load all types of bulk shipments. The St. Louis facility has a storage capacity of 5 million gallons with room for expansion to meet the needs of current and future customers. The terminal is equipped with a nitrogen transfer system that can handle loads from rail, truck, or barge. Slay Bulk Terminals has consistently received outstanding performance ratings in safety and environmental protection.

SI Warehousing is the parent company for a number of warehousing and packaged goods handling operations. One of its newest ventures is a contract packaging business near the Houston ship channel. The division receives bulk goods under contract from chemical plants and other manufacturers, then packages them for ocean-going vessels. Bi-State Warehousing, a regional division, offers storage space for palletized and non-palletized packaged goods as well as stenciling, labeling, banding, and repackaging services.

Cahokia Marine Service is a multimodal transportation complex located on the Mississippi River directly across from downtown St. Louis. The facility was formerly the site of an electric power plant and offers a unique, fully integrated transshipment service to and from barge, rail, truck, and storage. The terminal provides its own rail switching service to work with its rail serving lines: Gateway Western, Southern Pacific, Santa Fe, and Conrail. The location offers excellent access to the interstate highway system and provides users readily available, cost-efficient barge service.

Archway Fleeting and Harbor Service owns four harbor tugs and operates extensive fleeting areas in the Port of St. Louis. Archway's tugs specialize in breaking down and building tows. The company offers mooring capacity for more than 350 barges.

CIP Corporation is Slay Industries' newest division, created to support the transportation industry. Utilizing Slay's extensive experience, CIP specializes in the acquisition and leasing of locomotives and railroad cars.

Inland Maintenance Company is

an outgrowth that applies Slay Industries' expertise in construction and maintenance projects. Inland's team of skilled mechanics, electricians, pipefitters, carpenters, machine operators, welders, trained laborers, and project management are experienced in building new facilities and providing contract maintenance to the chemical, petrochemical, and utility industries.

Slay Industries is at the hub of the transportation industry in St. Louis. This natural advantage, coupled with depth of diversity and experience in the industry, positions Slay Industries as a quality provider of transportation services in the local,

RIGHT: Archway Fleeting and Harbor Service owns four harbor tugs and operates extensive fleeting areas in the Port of St. Louis.

BELOW: Slay Transportation operates more than 250 specialized trailers throughout the 48 contiguous states and portions of Canada.

national, and international arenas.

"Slay Industries has built its reputation on more than 60 years of meeting customers' needs for excellence in transportation," says Rhodes. "Today, we bring that same commitment of quality and safety to all of our transportation service enterprises and to all our customers. We will continue to do so as we grow into the future."

CHAPTER TEN

The Media

S t. Louis' various communication resources keep the area's residents entertained and informed.

St. Louis Post-Dispatch, 110

Photo by Terry Barner

St. Louis Post-Dispatch

ALWAYS FIGHT FOR PROGRESS AND REFORM, NEVER TOLERATE INJUSTICE OR CORRUPTION, ALWAYS FIGHT DEMAGOGUES OF ALL PARTIES, NEVER BELONG TO ANY PARTY, ALWAYS OPPOSE PRIVILEGED CLASSES AND PUBLIC PLUNDERERS, NEVER LACK SYMPATHY WITH THE POOR, ALWAYS REMAIN DEVOTED TO THE PUBLIC WELFARE, NEVER BE SATISFIED WITH MERELY PRINTING NEWS, ALWAYS BE DRASTICALLY INDEPENDENT, NEVER BE AFRAID TO ATTACK WRONG, WHETHER BY PREDATORY PLUTOCRACY OR PREDATORY POVERTY.

JOSEPH PULITZER

APRIL 10, 1907

Upon his retirement in 1907, Joseph Pulitzer set forth the *Post-Dispatch* Platform; more than 80 years later it is still the foundation upon which the paper is based.

Joseph Pulitzer moved to St. Louis in 1865 as a penniless Hungarian immigrant who had served briefly during the Civil War in the Union Army. But by 1878, after he had already achieved success as a reporter and a businessman, the 31-year-old Pulitzer bought the bankrupt *Evening Dispatch* for $2,500 at a public auction on the steps of the St. Louis Courthouse. The *Dispatch* almost immediately merged with the *Evening Post* and became the *St. Louis Post-Dispatch*.

The new paper pledged that it "will serve no party but the people... will oppose all frauds and shams whatever and wherever they are; will advocate principles and ideas rather than prejudices and partisanship."

In the years since then, the Pulitzer name has become synonymous with the highest standards of journalism. Columbia University's Pulitzer Prizes were created with an endowment from Joseph Pulitzer in 1903.

The *St. Louis Post-Dispatch* has been guided by the Pulitzer family for three generations. The first Joseph Pulitzer blazed a new trail in the world of journalism, founding a newspaper that not only printed the news, but served as a moral force mobilizing the power of reform. The second Joseph Pulitzer followed his father's trail with dedication and forcefulness that made the *Post-Dispatch* famous. The grandson—current chairman Joseph Pulitzer—carried on with vision that encompassed timely changes without departing from the basic course. More than 100 years have passed since the *Post-Dispatch* was founded, but time has not eroded the guiding principles of the paper's platform.

As the business of covering the news grew more complex, the Pulitzer Publishing Company evolved and expanded; the company has a long history of innovation. The *Post-Dispatch* was the first major metropolitan newspaper in the country to be printed by offset presses. The company founded its first radio station in 1922 and its first television station in 1947.

Today Pulitzer Publishing, a diversified media company, publishes two metropolitan newspapers: the *Post-Dispatch* and *The Arizona Daily Star* in Tucson, Arizona; and two suburban daily papers, the *Southtown Economist* and *The Daily Calumet* in Chicago, Illinois. The company also owns seven television stations and two radio stations in markets around the country.

The *Post-Dispatch* now employs more than 1,500 people. In addition to the downtown St. Louis plant, *Post* employees work at a suburban printing facility and an inserting site. The *Post* also operates 16 news bureaus, including one in Washington, D.C. Reporters and photographers travel around the world to bring to St. Louis stories of newsworthy events firsthand.

The look and content of the *Post-Dispatch* have changed over the past century. Now the paper includes a commentary page with a range of

viewpoints, including some different from those expressed on the editorial page. The Sunday *Post-Dispatch* magazine has been improved through redesign several times—most recently in 1987. In 1988-1989 the *Post* expanded its coverage of sports, neighborhood and suburban news, and business.

The *St. Louis Post-Dispatch* is regarded as one of the finest newspapers in the nation. High-quality color photographs are a standard feature of each issue. The paper is printed on six Goss Metro offset presses, each capable of printing 60,000 papers an hour. Reporters type their stories on video display terminals. Once in the computer's memory bank, a story can be retrieved for editing and typesetting. Even the *Post-Dispatch* reference library, which contains 12 million news clippings and close to 3 million photographs, has been automated so that when a reporter makes a request, a clipping is retrieved and displayed on a computer screen.

The *Post-Dispatch* continues to pursue an aggressive automation program. The newspaper is employ-

ing the latest digital-graphics technology with its Scitex color-imaging system. The Scitex system significantly reduces the time required to process color photographs, allowing later deadlines and better photo coverage of breaking news stories.

The *Post-Dispatch* recently opened a new inserting plant; this plant incorporates state-of-the-art palletizing equipment that can handle more than 10 million advertising inserts and newspaper sections each week.

The *Post* has also begun using a new low-rub ink formulation, which decreases ink rub-off by more than 80 percent. Readers no longer need to endure dirty fingers when reading the *Post-Dispatch.*

Throughout its history the *Post-Dispatch* has been committed to advanced technology while maintaining journalistic excellence. The result is a newspaper that most St. Louisans make a habit of reading. In 1990 *Post-Dispatch* circulation was close to 377,000 daily and 562,000 on Sundays. Nearly nine out of 10 people in the market read the *Post* each week. Over the past few years the *Post-Dispatch* has been one of the

The *St. Louis Post-Dispatch* offers a colorful variety of sections designed to appeal to its vast audience.

fastest growing metropolitan newspapers in the country. With its vast audience, the *Post* is the market's major advertising vehicle.

The *Post-Dispatch* has established a tradition of supporting the St. Louis community. For more than 40 years, the newspaper has conducted the 100 Neediest Cases campaign to raise money during the holiday season for thousands of families. And the *Post-Dispatch* maintains a commitment to education; each year, the paper sponsors the Scholar Athlete Awards, a spelling bee, a science fair, and the A-Student Program.

With a proud history, a commitment to progress, and high-quality journalism, the *Post-Dispatch* is set to serve the St. Louis community in the 1990s and beyond. The *St. Louis Post-Dispatch* is dedicated to meeting the challenges of the future, guided and inspired by the same principles that have made it successful for more than 110 years.

CHAPTER ELEVEN

Business and Professions

Greater St. Louis' business and professional community brings a wealth of service, ability, and insight to the area.

Blue Cross and Blue Shield of Missouri

The name sounds familiar, but the face looks a little different. Blue Cross and Blue Shield of Missouri (BCBSMo) sounds like a company that has been around forever, but this entity resulted from a merger of two companies in October 1986. The new corporation can claim to be the youngest as well as the most experienced health care-benefits financing company in Missouri.

But even that is a bit of misnomer: BCBSMo no longer merely offers health insurance. Today, as a reflection of the health care industry, BCBSMo concentrates on managing health benefits for companies.

To this concentration, BCBSMo brings 90 combined years of experience in financing health care from its

Blue Cross and Blue Shield of Missouri combines the advantages of an older, established company with a new company's willingness to experiment and innovate.

predecessor companies—Blue Cross Health Services Inc. and Missouri Medical Service. Blue Cross Health Services began in 1936, when even basic health care was a luxury for many. In 1945 Missouri Medical Service (Blue Shield) brought medical and surgical benefits to members.

Benefits management is the mechanism that will enable BCBSMo to carry out its mission of ensuring affordable access to quality care for its members in the 1990s and beyond. "Benefits management is absolutely vital," says Roy Heimburger, president and chief executive officer. "In an industry caught up now in two decades of all but constant change, no change has been more meaningful than the shift of health insurers from unquestioning payers for health care ser-

Roy Heimburger, president and chief executive officer of Blue Cross and Blue Shield of Missouri.

vices to participants in health care decision making—the change to managed benefits."

People hear the phrase "benefits management" and think of health maintenance organizations or preferred provider organizations. Managing benefits encompasses HMOs and PPOs, but it also includes benefit design, utilization review, and assessing quality. In addition, contracts with providers of health care, underwriting, and pricing all play a part in managing benefits. Managing benefits encourages efficiency while it requires that the same attention be devoted to assurance of quality as much as to control of cost, Heimburger adds.

Blue Cross and Blue Shield of Missouri employs nearly 1,600 people at its headquarters in St. Louis and regional offices in Jefferson City, Springfield, Cape Girardeau, and Kansas City. The company pays more than $2 billion a year in claims, including more than $1.5 billion in Medicare claims.

Armstrong, Teasdale, Schlafly, Davis & Dicus

With the 1989 merger of two law firms, the resulting firm of Armstrong, Teasdale, Schlafly, Davis & Dicus now spans the state of Missouri. And with the move into Metropolitan Square, the tallest building in Missouri, Armstrong, Teasdale, Schlafly, Davis & Dicus reaffirmed its long-standing commitment to downtown St. Louis.

The firm occupies three-and-one-half floors and will probably occupy five floors by 1994. That further symbolizes Armstrong, Teasdale's growth—the firm doubled in size between 1984 and 1989.

The combined law firms, comprised of 158 lawyers, stands as the fourth-largest firm based in the state. Thomas Remington, chairman of the law firm, does not see the growth stopping any time in the near future.

Since the merger, Armstrong, Teasdale has continued a strong practice in banking, bankruptcy,

Armstrong, Teasdale, made up of more than 150 lawyers, stands as the fourth-largest law firm in Missouri.

business litigation, education, and environmental law. For example, the firm represents Boatmen's 1st National Bank of Kansas City, Southwest Bank and Landmark Bank, the unsecured creditors in the Apex Oil Co. bankruptcy, and the St. Louis Community College District. Other clients include Anheuser-Busch Cos., Inc., McCarthy Brothers, Southwestern Bell Corporation, and Union Electric Co.

Specializing in civil work, Armstrong, Teasdale was founded in 1901. In addition to Kansas City, Armstrong, Teasdale maintains offices in Belleville, Illinois, and Overland Park, Kansas.

Armstrong, Teasdale's lawyers graduated from law schools ranging from Boston University to Yale and from the universities of Illinois and Missouri to Wake Forest. Many of the lawyers had legal experience before joining the firm, including judicial clerkships and government service; a number of them held careers in other fields before practicing law. The participate in bar association committees, pro bono matters, continuing legal education programs

and seminars, community organizations, and charitable organizations.

Armstrong, Teasdale offers a unique opportunity for lawyers who want a sophisticated and diverse practice. The firm is large enough and sufficiently specialized to handle complex legal issues and business planning concerns that confront its clients. At the same time, the firm has designed the organization to retain close personal relationships—both with clients and within the firm.

Each partner and associate is valued as an individual professional, not just an employee, in an ever-growing business. Armstrong, Teasdale strives to retain this blend of high-quality legal work with a friendly, enjoyable work atmosphere as the firm expands.

The firm comprises 17 departments, including litigation; railroad, aviation, and admiralty; labor; trusts and estates; financial restructuring, reorganization, and bankruptcy; real estate; intellectual property; and environmental law. It is one of the few general practice firms in the region to practice in the

RIGHT: The architecture firm of the Christner Partnership designed Armstrong, Teasdale's board room to reflect the firm's sophistication and professionalism.
Photo by William Mathis

BELOW: Visitors to Armstrong, Teasdale are afforded a view from the reception area into the firm's well-appointed library.
Photo by William Mathis

patent and trademark fields.

Five litigation lawyers are members of the American College of Trial Lawyers, and Armstrong, Teasdale has one of the most extensive trial practices of any firm in the state. In environmental law, Armstrong, Teasdale has counseled lessors, lessees, lenders, buyers, and sellers in transactions involving land with potential hazardous-waste problems

The employment relations practice includes representing national and local companies across the spectrum of a management-oriented labor practice, both for unionized and nonunionized employers. The firm's real estate lawyers have represented developers, landowners, and lenders in a wide range of complex matters such as providing service in projects involving downtown office towers, shopping malls, suburban and urban apartment complexes, as well as in farmland and other real estate projects in rural Missouri, Illinois, and Kansas.

Armstrong, Teasdale's bankruptcy practice has expanded rapidly in the past few years; it involves using sophisticated techniques—both within and outside the jurisdiction of the bankruptcy courts—to assist troubled companies or to represent substantial creditors. For example, Armstrong, Teasdale has represented a major national life insurance company on agricultural bankruptcy proceedings across the country.

The trust and estates department handles all matters requiring knowledge of state probate and trust law, as well as the law of federal estate, gift, and generation-skipping transfer taxes. Also, Armstrong, Teasdale historically has represented litigants in many prominent and significant cases in the area of patent, trademark, and intellectual property law. The firm negotiates licenses of patents, trademarks, copyrights, and trade secrets in technology on behalf of both domestic and offshore clients.

The nine remaining departments in Armstrong, Teasdale's practice have been combined into a business services group. This structure makes easier delivery of superior and timely services to its business clients. Practices included in this department are public and educational law; health care; international; computer law; tax law; corporate law; securities, banking, and financial services; employee benefits, pension, and executive compensation; and franchising.

Thomas Remington and Kenneth Teasdale, the firm's managing partner, both look out at the Mississippi River from the firm's offices in Metropolitan Square, pleased with what they see of the tradition that is St. Louis in their purview. And pleased, too, with how computer friendly the building is in accommodating the services clients need and expect.

But, they add, the view inside the firm is a solidly satisfying one, too.

Charles L. Crane Agency Co.

Since 1885 thousands of businesses and individuals have come to depend on the Charles L. Crane Agency for an unsurpassed level of insurance counseling and service. Over the years Crane has grown along with its clients by providing ideas specifically designed to meet their needs.

Crane clients have always had their own special reasons for choosing the agency. But in every case, the coverages provided fit their needs and the quality and level of service felt right. And in every case, Crane's primary goal has been to understand the client's needs in order to develop a sound program of risk management and insurance coverage.

The Charles L. Crane Agency is much more than simply a part of the St. Louis business community. By providing many of the city's leading companies with virtually every type of insurance, Crane has been a key ingredient in the growth of the community and the success of thousands of companies doing business many miles from St. Louis.

Crane, too, has grown over the years to become the oldest and one of the largest independently owned insurance agencies in the area. Today the agency serves more than 20,000 clients, ranging from local individuals and businesses to regional, national, and international accounts.

A number of Crane's clients have done business with the agency since before the turn of the century, and the average client has been with the agency for more than 15 years.

Locally the client list reads like a Who's Who of St. Louis' leading corporations and includes Missouri's largest bank, one of the community's primary utilities, and many St. Louis-based national and international corporations.

The Crane Agency is a member of

ABOVE: The Charles L. Crane Agency is uniquely positioned to provide its clients with a superior level of coverage and service.

RIGHT: Crane has a professional depth unmatched at many national and international insurance agencies.

InsGroup, a national network of 128 of the finest independent insurance agencies in America. Collectively this group represents $2.1 billion in annual property and casualty premiums. This association is testament to the agency's high standards and well-known commitment to excellence within the insurance industry.

The Crane Agency's offices overlook the St. Louis riverfront and each working day are home to well over 100 of America's finest insurance professionals.

With an average of 19 years experience, Crane's more than 40 independent agents are uniquely qualified to evaluate their clients' insurance requirements and to recommend the most effective and efficient solutions.

Crane's marketing department handles the critical task of finding the right insurance carrier and the best coverage to meet each set of insurance needs. Members of this department average 18 years of experience.

As a group, Crane agents specialize in a remarkably broad range of industries and coverages, providing insurance for everything from asbestos abatement contractors to zoos. Some of the agency's more unusual coverages include a circus, a major ski resort (including the mountain itself), and rain insurance for various outdoor concerts and festivals. This diversity of expertise means that whatever insurance needs one may have, the Crane agency is qualified to serve them.

At many agencies Crane's size, one becomes simply a "house account," and one's needs are served by whichever agent happens to be available. But Crane clients enjoy the benefits of a personal, working relationship with their agents.

Crane's size and stability are reflected in the fact that the agency represents virtually every major property and casualty insurance company in America. The agency represents 20 of America's largest insurance carriers and nearly an equal number of more specialized carriers and is privileged to have direct access to London and other specialty underwriters. This kind of depth is

The Crane Agency's offices are home to well over 100 of America's finest insurance professionals.

RIGHT and BELOW: Crane's more than 40 independent agents are well qualified to evaluate their clients' insurance requirements and to recommend the most effective and efficient solutions.

unmatched at many national and international insurance agencies.

While many of Crane's relationships with its carriers go back a long way (11 of them are 50 or more years old), others are practically brand new. The agency constantly seeks out specialized programs developed and offered by insurance companies that have not been previously represented.

The strength and length of Crane's relationships with these companies, along with the considerable abilities of its agents and support personnel, pay important dividends to its clients. They allow the Crane Agency to meet practically any insurance need with the most appropriate and cost-effective coverages possible.

Crane's professionals concentrate on quality in all areas, including

property and casualty insurance, workers' compensation programs, surety, employee benefits, life and health programs, claims and risk management consulting, and loss control. In many cases the agency serves its clients total commercial and personal insurance needs.

The Charles L. Crane Agency is uniquely positioned to provide its clients with a level of coverage and service unmatched anywhere in the industry.

Crane possesses the size and strength necessary to deliver the most effective and cost-efficient solutions to virtually every insurance need. At the same time its independence and long history of dedication to its clients produces a commitment to service usually found only in smaller, less sophisticated agencies.

This is why, for more than a century, thousands of businesses and individuals have chosen to trust their insurance needs to the Charles L. Crane Agency.

Thompson & Mitchell

Thompson & Mitchell was founded in 1929 as St. Louis' first full-service law firm. It was the first to offer extensive specialization, branch offices, and top-quality lawyers recruited from national, as well as local, law schools.

The foundation of the firm's practice was the city's largest corporation, Shell Oil Company, which was then headquartered in St. Louis. The firm grew rapidly to 40 lawyers, with branch offices in Houston and Tulsa. In addition, Sam Mitchell represented one of the city's major banks, Mercantile Trust Company, while Guy Thompson, after completion of a term as president of the American Bar Association, was appointed bankruptcy trustee of the Missouri Pacific Railroad.

Today Shell's headquarters are long gone, but the firm continues to represent Shell locally, as well as Mercantile's successor throughout Missouri. It also handles projects for Missouri Pacific's successor, the Union Pacific, throughout the nation. Indeed, Thompson & Mitchell has evolved into a major regional law firm—a firm capable of representing national corporations locally and local businesses nationally and internationally. While the firm's focus continues to be regional, its lawyers travel the nation and the world, representing the interests of clients in business transactions, in litigation matters, and in dealings with governments. Through mergers with well-established local firms, Thompson & Mitchell has extended its services to Washington, D.C.; Belleville, Illinois; and St. Charles, Missouri. With 175 lawyers, Thompson & Mitchell ranks as one of the two largest law firms headquartered in the state of Missouri.

Quality has been the hallmark of Thompson & Mitchell's legal work for more than six decades—an adherence to standards of practice comparable to those of the nation's largest and best-known law firms. The firm long ago achieved the goal of admission to the ranks of the most respected American firms. Recognition of that status by national, regional, and local clients has resulted in the firm's stature as one of the nation's 200 largest law firms.

Responsiveness is the first lesson taught to every new associate. The client's interests are first and foremost. Clients often select Thompson & Mitchell when time is of the essence. They know that the firm is large enough to staff their project in a way that assures deadlines will be met. The firm's objective is for all of its clients to know that their matters will be completed in a timely fashion, that communications will be smooth and constant, and that every lawyer assigned will devote the time and talent essential to attaining the client's objective.

Client relations are of great importance to the firm. Many of its clients have been counseled by the firm for decades on a wide variety of matters and consider Thompson & Mitchell to be an integral part of the team they assemble to achieve personal or business objectives. Thompson & Mitchell fosters this relationship by ensuring that each of its clients receives individual attention from one or a small group of attorneys. The firm's role is to understand the business of its client from a legal perspective, to supervise and be responsible for all of its work on the client's behalf, and to help the client avoid litigation and other problems.

Cost containment is an increasingly important client objective and one that Thompson & Mitchell seeks to help to achieve. The firm seeks to provide the leanest staffing on client matters consistent with high professional standards. It uses paralegals when possible, to give clients the benefit of their lower cost. It constantly searches for cost-effective solutions to clients' prob-

Thompson & Mitchell has been a part of the rebirth of downtown St. Louis. The firm occupies five upper floors of Mercantile Tower.

LEFT: Research is centered in the firm's modern and extensive library, equipped with the latest computer technology. Photo by Steven Goldstein Photography, Inc.

BELOW: The firm's conference rooms have served to close numerous major financial and business transactions. Photo by Steven Goldstein Photography, Inc.

the St. Louis and Washington offices. The Washington office includes experts in bank and financial institution regulation, employee benefits, insurance, international trade, legislation, and maritime finance, who supplement traditional areas of expertise in St. Louis.

Professional development enables Thompson & Mitchell lawyers to stay at the forefront of their respective fields. Its lawyers frequently speak to and write for business and professional groups on developments in the law. The firm relies on continuing legal education programs presented in-house, brought to its offices by satellite, or presented by professional organizations locally or around the country. Its extensive collection of legal literature is supplemented by computerized data bases that provide immediate access to the latest judicial and legislative developments.

Good citizenship has been an important component of Thompson & Mitchell's reputation from its beginning. Its lawyers have served as presidents of the St. Louis, the Missouri, and the American bar associations and as board heads of the University of Missouri, Washington University, and many charitable, educational, civic, and professional organizations. Partners have served as senators, congressmen, state supreme court judges, and other elected and appointed public officials.

lic finance and municipal law, real estate, international, labor, legislation, bankruptcy, health care, and environmental law. Its litigation department deals with commercial, antitrust, product liability, tort, maritime, railroad, and environmental litigation matters. Its tax department advises and represents individuals, partnerships, and corporations in state and federal tax matters and in employee benefit and executive compensation planning. Its estate planning department assists individuals with gift and estate planning and provides representation in connection with decedent estates.

Offices in Belleville and St. Charles each offer local clients not only the services of the largest local law firm but also the benefit of additional specialization available from

lems, whether they involve business, litigation, or personal matters. Thompson & Mitchell has been in the forefront of the movement to develop means of alternative dispute resolution short of actual litigation.

Expertise in many areas of specialization is fostered by Thompson & Mitchell's departmental organization. Its corporate department includes sections practicing in corporate and administrative law, corporate finance and securities, banking and financial institutions, commercial finance, pub-

CHAPTER TWELVE

Hospitality

S t. Louis visitors find comfort in the city's many fine accommodations.

Photo by Doug Adams/
Unicorn Stock Photos

Drury Inns, Inc.

The Drury Inn hotel system has grown from a small family plastering business in southeast Missouri to a steadily developing hotel chain with an eye on customer needs for quality and value.

The Drury concept evolved when the Drury family found a way to keep hotel operation simple. By eliminating restaurants, convention facilities, and many of the frills typically found in pricey hotels, they were able to offer quality hotel accommodations at rates 25 to 30 percent below full-service hotels. This concept has helped Drury rank high—both in the lodging industry and with guests.

Giving up the frills has meant no sacrifice in hospitality. Drury Inn hotels offer a free *QUIKSTART*® break-

fast where guests may have fresh fruit, cereal, toast, pastries, and beverages. Drury Inn guests may watch cable television, make free local telephone calls, swim in the pool, and request nonsmokers' rooms. And special-rate programs are available for frequent travelers, corporations, groups, and senior citizens.

This common sense approach did not eliminate quality. Drury Inns are constructed according to rigid standards. In fact, 90 percent of Drury Inn hotels qualify for AAA's three-diamond rating. The Drury organization also operates a small chain of quality budget hotels under the Thrifty Inn name.

St. Louis is the hub for the Drury

system, which now includes more than 60 hotels and motels. In addition to nine Drury Inn hotels, three Thrifty Inns, and a Hampton Inn in the St. Louis area, Drury Inns, Inc., calls St. Louis home to its operations office, located near the Lambert-St. Louis International Airport. The southeast Missouri roots are kept intact with support

functions, such as purchasing, accounting, and a reservation center, located in Cape Girardeau.

A unique product in the Drury chain can be found in St. Louis. The Drury Inn hotel of Union Station is a striking renovation of a 1907 YMCA, which offered a haven to railroad workers. Another innovative project involves the construction of a Drury Inn hotel atop historic Union Market, located directly adjacent to St. Louis Convention Center. Indoor pools and whirlpools and distinctive public areas are highlights of both hotels.

Development plans include continued expansion of the company's own Drury Inn and Thrifty Inn concepts, and operation of other brands, such as Hampton Inns, both for the company and for outside owners.

RIGHT and BELOW: Drury Inn hotels offer top-quality accommodations with reasonable rates at more than 40 convenient locations.

The Breckenridge Frontenac Hotel and Conference Center

One can learn a lot at a cocktail party if one just keeps one's ears open. Listening to guests in the relaxed atmosphere of the weekly cocktail parties at The Breckenridge Frontenac Hotel and Conference Center has resulted in the change to softer colors in the rooms, minisuites that allow privacy as well as togetherness, and healthy food on the menus.

"We really listen to our guests," says Patricia Brett-Bergauer, general manager. "We try to get to know our guests by name and pay attention to

The Breckenridge Frontenac Hotel and Conference Center is a corporate hotel during the week and a social setting on weekends.

their opinions. When we renovated recently, we painted the rooms in colors such as mauve because the guests suggested they wanted their rooms to be soothing."

Constant travelers told hotel personnel that they would like to exercise but were on the road so much that they never had the chance to learn to use the equipment properly, so The Breckenridge Frontenac provides a trainer in its health club that is open seven days a week for guests.

The Breckenridge Frontenac is an independent hotel that opened in 1974. The establishment of 310 guest rooms is a corporate hotel during the week, but it becomes a social setting on the weekends. The hotel

FACING PAGE: The hotel includes 22,000 square feet of meeting space.

includes 22,000 square feet of meeting space, with the largest measuring 10,045 square feet, divisible in many ways. Meetings fill the large and small rooms during the week, but on the weekends, the same spaces accommodate bridal showers, bridge parties, and weddings, as well as meetings.

"Because we're so close to several residential areas, the location is conducive to social activities, such as housing all the guests for weddings," says Brett-Bergauer. "They stay here, but can get to and from the hostess' house easily." Especially appealing to such a party is Frontenac Towers, the hotel within a hotel, with 56 rooms and 32 suites with wet bars and parlors.

For the business traveler the executive registry includes the services of a concierge, a library, a large-screen television, a bar, and turndown service with a bathrobe, mints, and a choice of 12 liqueurs. The Breckenridge Frontenac and Conference Center employs 250 people to shine the crystal, drive guests to nearby Plaza Frontenac for shopping, check out books from the library, and listen to guests' suggestions for the hotel.

Henry VIII Hotel and Conference Center

Henry VIII stands pompous and tubby at the foot of the sweeping stairs at the inn named for him. Even in colored glass he is a presence, promising bountiful tables, grand entertainment, and courtly behavior.

The inn bearing his name, the Henry VIII Hotel and Conference Center, rises near Lambert-St. Louis International Airport. Wood traces the lines of the building, keeping with the Tudor style of sixteenth-century England, when Henry ruled. Henry VIII Hotel is an independently owned property.

With advantageous proximity to the major airport, the hotel sits on a hill surrounded by greenery and laced with paths for jogging and walking. Tennis courts and indoor and outdoor pools are available.

Inside, the hotel is comprised of 400 sleeping rooms (half of which are large suites), two restaurants, three lounges, and 27 meeting rooms—all almost as spacious as a castle.

The restaurant known as Henry VIII has won the coveted Travel Holiday Award four times. The restaurant, decorated in royal red colors and dark wood, serves robust meals of American cuisine, with steaks and prime rib prominent. The second restaurant is Duffy's, an Irish pub serving lunch and dinner—including corned beef and cabbage—in a room dotted with antiques such as an old brass National cash register and a grand wooden bar that once served as the front desk before the hotel was expanded.

The lobby serves as a hub from which the meeting rooms radiate; at the center of the lobby is a crystal chandelier. Crystal also shines from the ceiling of the ballroom—11,000 square feet of space that can be divided into five rooms for conferences. The Henry VIII Hotel and Conference Center's meeting and conference rooms can accommodate groups of 10 as well as groups of 1,500.

Under new management Henry VIII Hotel and Conference Center has been restored to its original charm, reflecting the needs of today's travelers.

CHAPTER THIRTEEN

Health

S t. Louis' many modern medical facilities make sure that visitors and residents receive the finest health care possible.

Photo by Cathy Ferris

Barnes Hospital

From far across the city of St. Louis, the lighted sign for Barnes Hospital shines. The sight comforts those on the way to the hospital, telling them that help is near.

Barnes Hospital sits across Kingshighway from Forest Park; many rooms face flowers and trees in the middle of the city. The venerable hospital celebrated its 75th anniversary in 1989, having opened its doors on December 7, 1914. The hospital followed a bequest by merchant Robert A. Barnes, who died in 1892.

In nearly a century of service, Barnes has ranked as one of the nation's premier hospitals, taking a place alongside Johns Hopkins, Massachusetts General, and Sanford. The St. Louis hospital, licensed for 1,208 beds, has been cited as one of the country's five best hospitals. This is no small feat in a nation that has more than 6,000 hospitals.

Barnes serves as a teaching hospital for the Washington University School of Medicine. This union had produced 17 Nobel prize winners by the hospital's 75th anniversary. The partnership also provides tremendous depth of resources and medical expertise for Barnes patients.

All doctors at Barnes are also board certified or board eligible in their specialities and areas of care. Barnes has more than 1,000 doctors on its staff.

At Barnes there are a dozen intensive care units. A patient with a head injury is cared for in a different intensive care unit from a patient who has suffered a heart attack or one who is fighting cancer.

Barnes is a leading organ-transplant hospital. Its surgeons have transplanted more than 1,000 kidneys since the program began in 1963, more than 140 hearts since 1985, and more than 100 livers since 1985. More than 50 lungs have been transplanted since that program began in 1988.

The hospital is a leader in new "minimally invasive" surgical techniques, including a surgical technique for gallstones, a problem afflicting about 20 million Americans.

The nonprofit hospital budgets more than $15 million a year for charity care.

It is the depth of medical expertise and the technology that make Barnes a national leader in health care. It is the Barnes commitment to St. Louis that makes it a tremendous resource for the patients of the community.

ABOVE: Five patients who received organ transplants from a single donor.

LEFT: Barnes Hospital, which is licensed for 1,208 beds, is one of the five leading hospitals in the nation. The hospital is located in the heart of St. Louis and is bordered by beautiful Forest Park.

BELOW: A lighted, contemporary pedestrian walkway links the Barnes subsurface parking garage to the hospital, offering safe and easy access to visitors.

St. Luke's Hospital

The founders of St. Luke's Hospital, who converted a Soulard mansion into a hospital in 1866, would be astonished by the present-day medical complex in Chesterfield, Missouri. The not-for-profit hospital, named for the patron saint of physicians, is located on 60 acres near Highway 40 on Woods Mill Road. St. Luke's has grown along with the developing residential and business community it serves in west St. Louis County.

Residents have depended on St. Luke's Hospital for exceptional cardiac care, laser surgery, cancer treatment, orthopedics, pediatrics, neurosurgery, and maternity care. The hospital's medical staff includes about 700 physicians in more than 30 specialties who provide a full range of services for area families.

The heart of St. Luke's Hospital is its dedication to excellent patient care. Throughout its 124 years St. Luke's has kept pace with changing medical technology. St. Luke's was the first hospital in St. Louis County to offer labor, delivery, recovery, and postpartum (LDRP) suites. These special delivery suites, which opened in July 1989, offer modern technology and family-centered maternity care with many of the comforts of home. Specially trained nurses care for both mother and

baby and teach parenting skills. Neonatologists, pediatricians, and nurses care for infants with special needs in the Special Care Nursery.

A perinatologist (an obstetrician specializing in high-risk pregnancies) serves as St. Luke's chief of obstetrics/gynecology. A hot line is answered 24 hours a day for parents who have questions or concerns about their babies. St. Luke's Division of Reproductive Endocrinology and Infertility provides comprehensive infertility evaluations.

Preventive medicine is another commitment of St. Luke's Hospital. St. Luke's Institute for Health Education offers a variety of educational programs, health screenings, and seminars for physicians, patients, employees, corporations, and the community in the Emerson Auditorium and adjacent conference rooms. More than 200,000 people have attended programs between December 1986, when the institute opened, and 1989. The institute is located in a five-story atrium between the hospital's two medical office buildings. A third medical office building on St. Luke's campus is planned for completion in spring 1991.

St. Luke's medical services extend outside the walls of the hospital in Chesterfield. The staff at St. Luke's Urgent Care Centers in Ballwin and Ellisville and at St. Luke's Health Center in Wentzville treat minor injuries and illnesses—from diagnosis and treatment to follow-up care. No appointment is necessary. Patients have access to the full resources of St. Luke's Hospital if more intensive care is needed.

Surrey Place, St. Luke's skilled nursing and residential care facility that opened at Olive Boulevard and Ladue Road in January 1990, and Generations Ahead, an older-adult resource center at the hospital expanded St. Luke's family-centered services. Surrey Place includes 120 fully licensed beds attended by

BELOW LEFT: St. Luke's Hospital is located on 60 landscaped acres in west St. Louis County.

BELOW RIGHT: The Drury family welcomes their new baby in one of St. Luke's special delivery suites.

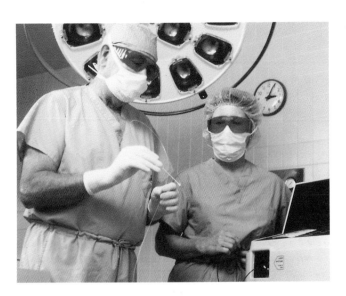

Today about 100 qualified physicians perform more than 1,400 laser procedures each year at St. Luke's Laser Institute.

skilled nurses, as well as a wing of 20 private, residential care rooms. The facility is located on a wooded bluff overlooking the Missouri River. Education programs for Surrey Place staff, residents, and families are presented regularly.

State-of-the-art medical technology is available at St. Luke's Laser Institute, the premier provider of laser surgery in the St. Louis area. About 100 St. Luke's physicians are qualified to perform laser procedures in several surgical specialties, including obstetrics/gynecology, ophthalmology, otolaryngology (ear, nose, and throat), and cancer treatment. In 1989 more than 1,400 laser procedures were done, most in St. Luke's expanded outpatient surgery department.

Patients with chronic renal disease receive convenient, out-patient hemodialysis treatment at the Affiliated Hospitals Dialysis Center in Creve Coeur. The center, which has 24 dialysis stations and rooms for home training, is a joint venture between St. Luke's and St. John's.

St. Luke's Radiation Oncology Center, which opened in 1977, is one of St. Louis' most advanced facilities. Each year the Radiation Oncology Center sees 400 new cancer patients and provides more than 9,500 treatments. St. Luke's Cancer Information Center offers information about cancer diagnosis, treatment, coping techniques, and support groups.

Women can receive physical examinations, mammography testing, and instruction in breast self-examination through the Breast Diagnostic Center, a specialized unit focusing on early detection of breast cancer. Low-dose mammogram screenings are performed in St. Luke's Mobile Mammography Unit, which travels throughout the St. Louis area. Specialists in gynecologic oncology diagnose and treat women with precancerous or cancerous conditions.

To treat people with drug and alcohol problems, St. Luke's Renew program provides outpatient counseling and therapy. Renew offers effective and cost-efficient treatment for chemical dependency, incorporating the most advanced techniques.

St. Luke's Ambulatory Care Center, located in the city's central west end, provides high-quality medical care to area residents, regardless of their ability to pay. St. Luke's Episcopal/Presbyterian Charitable Fund was established to finance programs for health care among the disadvantaged.

The most advanced medical treatment, excellent patient care, health education, and beautiful surroundings are all hallmarks of St. Luke's Hospital, a leader in health care for St. Louis families since 1866.

Medical conferences and education programs for the community are held in the 275-seat auditorium in St. Luke's Institute for Health Education.

DePaul Health Center

The landing gear on the plane failed. Everyone at the airport stood on alert for the wounded plane to land. A few miles away at DePaul Health Center everyone waited on alert, too, ready to care for the injured if the worst should happen. It did not. But being ready defines the services at DePaul for emergencies, for long-term illnesses, and for the joy of birth or recuperation.

DePaul Health Center has come a long way from the three-room log cabin at Fourth and Spruce streets in St. Louis. Now located at the intersection of interstates 70 and 270 in St. Louis County, the 607-bed hospital is now the oldest existing Catholic hospital in the United States and part of the Daughters of Charity National Health System, the largest nonprofit health system in the nation.

In 1828 DePaul was the first

Catholic hospital west of the Mississippi River. From the beginning the St. Louis business community has supported the healers. For example, land for the first hospital was donated by John Mullanphy, a local merchant. Following that hospital came a children's home and a hospital for psychiatric patients.

St. Vincent's Asylum, opened in 1858, was an innovation. Instead of merely housing the mentally ill, the Daughters of Charity treated the disorder. DePaul continues to serve as an innovator in the field of psychiatry as well as in a variety of other specialties.

Currently one of the oldest and largest psychiatric hospitals in America, the St. Vincent's division of DePaul Health Center offers mental health services to children, adolescents, adults, and older adults. In

DePaul Health Center's Cancer Treatment Center features the newest and most advanced diagnostic and cancer treatment programs.

addition, a stress program allows individuals who are struggling with an excessive amount of stress to receive help and return to good physical and psychological health.

Heart disease is the most frequent cause of death for adults in the United States today, and the St. Louis Heart Institute provides a coordinated program for area businesses, individuals, and other providers of health services. Because accurate diagnosis is the key to quick recovery, the team at DePaul offers a variety of sophisticated diagnostic tests to detect coronary artery disease, valve malfunction, heart muscle weakness, and other conditions. DePaul's heart program offers treatment in the form of medicine, angioplasty, surgery, and transplantation followed by a comprehensive rehabilitation program.

The cancer treatment program at DePaul provides an individual approach to the prevention, diagnosis, and treatment of cancer through a combination of high technology and tenderness. A team approach using the expertise of a variety of specialists ensures that cancer patients and their families are given the maximum support in fighting this complex and emotionally devastating disease.

In orthopedics DePaul combines quality medical care with research and training. The biomechanical laboratory has pioneered new devices and techniques for anchoring artificial hip and knee joints, which are now used throughout the world. In addition, DePaul performs other procedures, such as sports medicine, spinal surgery, and microsurgery on nerves and veins.

One of the newer services at DePaul is the laser program, one of the most advanced in the Midwest. The word "laser" is an acronym of "light amplification by the stimulated emission of radiation"; and with more than 13 lasers, varying in color, strength, and capability, doctors at DePaul gain the maximum from technology, thereby cutting costs and improving surgery. Lasers are painless medical tools—infinitely more precise than even the sharpest surgery scalpel—and can be used, among other ways, to vaporize cancerous growth, cauterize bleeding ulcers, alleviate pelvic pain and infertility, and eliminate wine-colored birthmarks.

Among these advances in health care, DePaul has piloted a program using bedside computer terminals. These computers aid with the flow of information about a patient, and when the machines are right in the room with the patient—rather than down the hall at the nurses' station—the physicians, nurses, and other medical personnel are able to enter and retrieve information regarding a patient's condition rapidly. That is becoming vitally important as patients stay fewer days. The bedside computer also allows the nursing staff to spend more time with patients and less time with charts and papers.

DePaul Health Center offers other services, including substance abuse, home health care, maternity and children's services, outpatient services, pain management, and rehabilitation programs, as well as standing by in case of emergencies at the nearby airport.

BELOW LEFT: The yellow-pulse dye laser allows physicians to treat port wine stains (birthmarks), with almost no danger of scarring, on children before they reach school age and before they begin to suffer the psychological trauma sometimes associated with these birthmarks.

BELOW RIGHT: At DePaul Health Center quality nursing care has been a hallmark for nearly 170 years. Today the tradition of caring continues as nurses provide skilled services in a highly technical environment, and yet they find the time to provide invaluable bedside care.

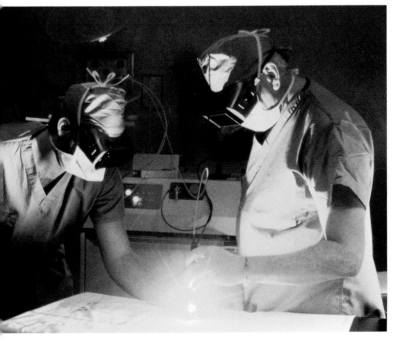
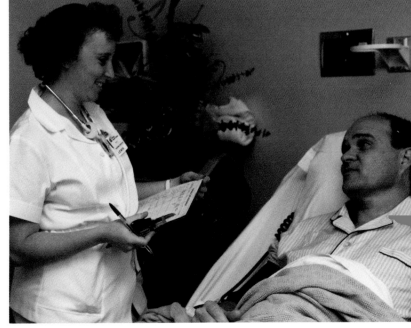

Deaconess Health Services

As Deaconess enters its second 100 years of service, it is steadfast in honoring its mission: Life of quality for all through value-centered health care and health education offered in the compassionate Spirit of Jesus Christ. "Our mission is what ties so many different and talented people together at Deaconess," says Richard P. Ellerbrake, president and chief executive officer.

Excellence and diversity at Deaconess are evident in many ways. Medical staff physicians are required to be board certified or be actively pursuing such credentials. A recent report documented that Deaconess had a higher percentage of board-certified physicians than any other hospital in Missouri.

The Deaconess College of Nursing, which has for years provided exemplary health care education, continues to enjoy strong enrollment. Standards in scholarship are high; the college is accredited by the North Central Association of Colleges and Schools. More than 2,200 of its graduates have gone into hospitals and other care facilities here, throughout the United States, and abroad. The current curriculum offers a four-year program leading to a bachelor of science in nursing and, for licensed practical nurses, an associate degree program. Students experience an eclectic approach to community teaching in an atmosphere that is personal and warm.

Another tradition at Deaconess, the Emergency Department, continues to serve thousands of people annually. It stands alert to provide needed health care 24 hours daily, year-round. Residents and visiting hotel guests alike can feel confident in choosing Deaconess for urgent care or information.

As a responsible citizen in the community, Deaconess is a leader in creating programs to keep health costs low. It was the first institution in St. Louis to offer a Preferred Provider Organization (PPO). The Deaconess Occupational Health Network (OHN) brings quality care to industry. These and other forward-looking activities express the Deaconess concern for the community's financial and physical well-being.

The Deaconess SurgiCenter for outpatient surgery is distinguished by availability of high-tech services and a quiet, confident ambiance. Designed for patients who do not need hospitalization, the SurgiCenter has received a high degree of community acceptance. It has grown rapidly in stature as one of the busiest facilities of its kind in the St. Louis area.

The Park Central Institute is another important part of the Deaconess medical campus. Its staff is comprised of highly trained physicians of world-class qualifications, who devote their skills to cosmetic facial surgery, reconstruction of the head and neck, and a complete

RIGHT: The Deaconess hemodialysis program serves many individuals from throughout the St. Louis area.

BELOW: Deaconess' mission is life of quality for all through value-centered health care and health education offered in the compassionate Spirit of Jesus Christ.

range of specialized ear, nose, and throat care.

The Deaconess Institute for Chemical Dependencies provides 24-hour, year-round intervention for persons suffering crises of alcohol and/or drug abuse.

Deaconess has the second-largest hemodialysis program in the St. Louis area, with 18 chronic and six inpatient units at the hospital, and 18 chronic plus one isolation unit at Deaconess South Dialysis Center in south St. Louis County.

The Deaconess Cardiac Catheterization Laboratory performs an average of 40 procedures each month.

The Deaconess Sleep Disorders and Research Center was the first of its kind in Missouri. It remains the largest. Its services include diagnoses and treatment of patients with sleep related problems, including difficulties in falling asleep, and staying asleep or remaining awake. The staff also is involved in many sleep-related research projects.

The internationally prominent *BASH*™ Treatment and Research Center for Eating and Mood Disorders is located at Deaconess. It is one of the largest such programs in the world, treating anorexia and bulimia nervosa as well as other eating disorders and mood problems.

Deaconess' Family Medicine residency program and treatment center serves every member of the family. Grandchildren, parents, and grandparents can receive care from the same physician. Services include obstetrics, infant and child care, elder care, counseling, health screening, minor surgery, and sports medicine.

Deaconess maintains a strong commitment to those who need assistance or additional therapy after they are discharged from the hospital. Deaconess Home Health

Services is available 24-hours daily to house-bound patients.

The Saint Louis Crisis Nursery is located at Deaconess Hospital. It has served more than 1,500 children since it was founded in 1986 by the Junior League of St. Louis, the Coalition of 100 Black Women, and Deaconess. The nursery is an independent not-for-profit agency offering temporary shelter for

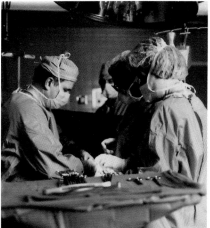

children from birth to six years old whose families are experiencing crises such as illness, death, overwhelming stress, or loss of housing.

President Ellerbrake sees the Deaconess mission in coming years as especially pertinent to the aging population. Today, on the brink of the twenty-first century, people live to be much older than they did in 1889, when Deaconess was founded. "This older population is going to be healthier longer than previous generations, and more independent," he says.

Many Deaconess medical capabilities have been augmented or revised to more effectively accommodate mature adults. In addition, a new

ABOVE: Deaconess provides health care for all family members.

LEFT: The hospital's surgical facilities include the Deaconess SurgiCenter for outpatient care.

program designed especially for adults 55 and older has been created. Named Senior Spirit, it is offered without dues. Members are invited to participate in a wide range of activities that includes health screenings, lectures and seminars, and social events. Members also are assisted in understanding their medical bills and in locating appropriate community resources.

Deaconess will continue to seek new ways to serve the community's well-being, both in response to existing health care needs and in pursuit of health-maintaining education and activities.

The future for Deaconess, says Ellerbrake, means using vision for science and tradition for compassion toward the community. "Today's health care field is complex and challenging, and the Deaconess family is called ever onward and upward by a commitment that is fresh every day."

Christian Health Services

The Christian Health System is a nonsectarian organization whose roots date back to the early 1900s, when the Christian Women's Benevolent Association founded Christian Hospital of St. Louis. Today a parent organization—Christian Health Services—serves as the umbrella for four operating companies: Christian Hospital Northeast/Northwest, CH Allied Services, CH Health Technologies, and Village North. The system's four companies deliver services in the areas of acute-care hospitals, long-term care, and diversified health services.

The Christian Health System has a mission and a vision: to be the premier not-for-profit health care system in Missouri and southern Illinois. The system—an integration of physicians and institutions—provides comprehensive health care that is economically efficient and strives to achieve superior quality in the outcome of patient care, as well as to promote good health and sat-

isfy the needs of the system's patients and customers.

The system's highly valued employees and partners accomplish this charitable mission through the use of advanced technologies and intelligent strategies of business. The amalgamation of medicine and business has been successfully achieved by Fred L. Brown, president and chief executive officer of Christian Health Services, the nonprofit and nonsectarian company that manages the system. Brown holds an undergraduate degree in

psychology and a master's degree in health care administration from George Washington University in Washington, D.C.

When he came to Christian Health Services in 1982, he strongly believed that executives in his field were becoming too "one-dimensional." Their training did not place enough emphasis on marketing and profitable enterprises, he said. So he began to hire professionals in business administration as well as in health care. Integration required one year.

"Health care people bring an un-

The Christian Health System's largest hospital is divided into two campuses—Christian Hospital Northeast (BELOW) and Christian Hospital Northwest (RIGHT).

LEFT: The Hedrick Medical Center in Chillicothe, Missouri, is one of the Christian Health System's greatest successes.

RIGHT: Fred L. Brown is the president and chief executive officer of Christian Health Services.

derstanding of the needs of the community," he says, adding that business executives bring their knowledge of management, finance, marketing, and data systems to the organization.

The results? During Brown's tenure the following changes have taken place. Gross revenues have risen from $85 million in 1982 to more than $400 million. The 728 beds in 1982 have increased to 2,057 beds. The two hospitals in 1982 have increased to nine. The once-struggling Hedrick Medical Center in Chillicothe, Missouri, has become one of the nation's biggest rural-hospital success stories.

Smart Solutions, a nutritional consulting division of the for-profit company, CH Health Technologies, is now the nation's largest consultant to nursing homes. Christian Hospital Northeast/Northwest's Emergency Department served about 70,000 visitors—one of the busiest emergency rooms in Missouri.

Christian Health System's largest hospital, Christian Northeast/Northwest provides tertiary care on two campuses in north St. Louis County—one in Florissant and one at the intersection of Interstate 270 and Highway 367. The two campuses resulted from near-constant expansion in the 1960s and 1970s.

Christian Hospital was founded in 1903 with 12 beds, the manifestation of Fannie H. S. Ayers' lifelong dream. She and other members of the Christian Woman's Benevolent Association had worked for years to provide medical care for the people of north St. Louis. The first hospital sat near the city's western boundary, but like the population, the hospital continued to move west until it crossed the county line in the 1960s.

Christian Hospital Northeast/Northwest has developed programs and services for its community, including home health care and hospice care, hospital-based ambulance service, reference laboratory services, management for medical office buildings, child-development programs, banquet rooms and auditoriums, gymnasiums for employee fitness, enhancements for physicians' practices, a directory of doctors for people without a physician, and a support system for people living at home alone.

Today the hospital system continues to grow, not by building new sites, but by expanding its acute-care and long-term care operations into a 150-mile radius. The system is buying, leasing, managing, or affiliating with hospitals and nursing homes in the area.

"We need to provide some assistance to smaller, rural hospitals," Brown says. "It's not just to increase our referrals. The fee we receive from managing those facilities is enough. We have a personal concern to help these smaller hospitals survive."

Over the past few years Brown has been recruiting physicians as part of an aggressive program to support specialists by bringing in more physicians who provide primary care. The staff at Christian Northeast/Northwest, for example, rose 28 percent, from 384 to 493 people, between 1985 and 1988. As incentives, Christian Health Systems offers marketing support through the doctors' directory and supplies health insurance for the physicians and their office staffs.

Brown continues to set an example of leadership. He has become a leading spokesman on health care and its business as chairman of the Missouri Hospital Association. In addition, he is a member of the American Hospital Association's Council on Management and leads a task force for governing for the American College of Healthcare Executives.

"A friend once told me that to achieve what you need to achieve, you must move out of your conservative position," Brown says. "I've made my move."

Patrons

The following individuals, companies, and organizations have made a valuable commitment to the quality of this publication. Windsor Publications gratefully acknowledges their participation in *St. Louis: Gateway to Tomorrow.*

Armstrong, Teasdale, Schlafly, Davis & Dicus*
Barnes Hospital*
Blue Cross and Blue Shield of Missouri*
The Breckenridge Frontenac Hotel and Conference Center*
Christian Health Services*
Charles L. Crane Agency Co.*
Deaconess Health Services*
DePaul Health Center*
Drury Inns, Inc.*
Henry VIII Hotel and Conference Center*
Nooter Corporation*
Pet Incorporated*

St. Louis Post-Dispatch*
St. Luke's Hospital*
Slay Industries*
Sunnen Products Co.*
Thompson & Mitchell*

*Participants in Part Two, "St. Louis' Enterprises." The stories of these companies and organizations appear in chapters 9 through 13, beginning on page 96.

138

Bibliography

"The Anatomy of an Accounting Firm." *Commerce*, August 1988, pp. 11-16.

"An Assessment of the St. Louis Region: Business Opportunities at the Nation's Population and Market Center" (The Fantus Report). *Commerce*, May 1989, pp. 43-61.

Burnett, Betty. *St. Louis at War: The Story of a City 1941-45*. Patrice Press, 1987.

Craig, Andrew B. "The Current Banking Environment," *Commerce*, June 1988, pp. 6-9.

"Decking the Malls." *Commerce*, May 1989, pp. 74-75.

Eliot, Stephen A. "Trends in Insurance: Setting a Course for the 1990s." *Commerce*, February 1989, pp. 24-25.

"Facing the Competition." *Commerce*, February 1989, pp. 31-33.

Faherty, William B., S.J. *St. Louis Portrait*. Continental Heritage, 1978.

————. *Henry Shaw: His Life and Legacies*. University of Missouri Press, 1987.

Faltermayer, Edmund. "How St. Louis Turned Less Into More." *Fortune*, December 23, 1985.

Fiala, Kenneth. "The Future of the Savings Institution Business." *Commerce*, June 1988, pp. 13-16.

Fifield, Barringer. *Seeing Saint Louis*. St. Louis: Washington University Press, 1987.

Fisher, Henry N.D. "Grand Old Landmark Returns to Glory." *Commerce*, October 1985.

Ford, Richard. "An Inside Look at the Venture Capital Business." *Commerce*, June 1988, pp. 25-27.

Franzwa, Gregory M. *The Old Cathedral*. Patrice Press, 1980.

"Growth is the Game Plan." *Commerce*, February 1989, pp. 7-9.

Hannon, Bob, ed. *St. Louis: Its Neighbors and Neighborhoods*. St. Louis: RCGA, 1987.

"Health Care." *St. Louis Business Journal*, June 19-25, 1989.

Horgan, James. *City of Flight*. Patrice Press, 1984.

Hunter, Julius. *Westmoreland and Portland Places*. Columbia: University of Missouri Press, 1988.

"It's Prime Time for Radio." *Commerce*, August 1988, pp. 19-22.

"Keeping Today's Hospitals Healthy Calls for Strong Medicine." *Commerce*, April 1988, pp. 37-40

"Koplar Communications, Inc., Loads the Bases." *Commerce*, July 1989, pp. 49-51.

"A Major St. Louis Player." *Commerce*, August 1988, pp. 7-8.

McCue, George. *The Building Art in St. Louis: Two Centuries*. St. Louis: AIA Foundation, 1981.

"Most Affordable Housing Market in America." *Commerce* Magazine, September 1988.

The Original Book of St. Louis Business 1989. St. Louis Business Journal, 1989.

"Playing the Numbers Game." *Commerce*, August 1988, pp. 25-30.

Primm, James Neal. *Lion of the Valley*. Pruett, 1981.

St. Louis Business Journal. Special issue on banking in St. Louis, June 19-25, 1989.

St. Louis Currents: The Community and Its Resources. Leadership St. Louis, 1986

Stith, Ann Carter. "Criminal Justice," in *St. Louis Currents: The Community and Its Resources*. Leadership St. Louis, 1986.

Troen, Selwyn K., and Glen E. Holt. *St. Louis*. New Viewpoints, 1977.

"Who's Making Waves in the Ad Agency Arena." *Commerce*, February 1989, pp. 14-17.

INTERVIEWS

Ina Boone, director, NAACP

Terry Ferris, St. Louis city planner

Glen Holt, director, St. Louis Public Library

Tom Irwin, St. Louis Economic Development Corporation

Dee Joyner, director, St. Louis County Economic Council

Bob Kelley, St. Louis Labor Council

Donald Lasater, former CEO, Mercantile Bancshares

Ellen O'Brien, president, St. Louis Realtors Association

James O'Flynn, president, AAA, former president, RCGA

Ed Ruesing, Downtown St. Louis Association

OTHER SOURCES

Boatmen's Bancshares

Clayton Chamber of Commerce

County Economic Development Office

Famous-Barr

Federal Reserve Eighth District

The Legends

Mayor's Office

NAACP

RCGA

St. Louis Business Journal

St. Louis Post-Dispatch

St. Louis Public Schools

St. Louis Realtors Association

Directory of Corporate Sponsors

Armstrong, Teasdale, Schlafly,
  Davis & Dicus, 114-115
  One Metropolitan Square
  St. Louis, MO 63102-2740
  314/621-5070
  Thomas R. Remington

Barnes Hospital, 127
  One Barnes Hospital Plaza
  St. Louis, MO 63110
  314/362-1327
  John Miller

Blue Cross and Blue Shield of
  Missouri, 113
  4444 Forest Park
  St. Louis, MO 63108
  314/658-4762
  Ed P. Egger

The Breckenridge Frontenac Hotel
  and Conference Center, 122-123
  1335 South Lindbergh
  St. Louis, MO 63131
  314/993-1100
  Patricia Brett-Bergauer

Christian Health Services, 134-135
  1155 Dunn Road
  St. Louis, MO 63136
  314/355-2300
  Tess Niehaus

Charles L. Crane Agency Co.,
  116-117
  100 South Fourth Street
  St. Louis, MO 63102
  314/241-8700
  Pierce W. Powens, Jr.

Deaconess Health Services, 132-133
  6150 Oakland Avenue
  St. Louis, MO 63139
  314/768-3000
  Gary Groh

DePaul Health Center, 130-131
  12303 DePaul Drive
  Bridgeton, MO 63044
  314/344-6000
  Cheryl S. Karn

Drury Inns, Inc., 121
  10801 Pear Tree Lane
  St. Louis, MO 63074
  314/429-2255
  Charles L. Drury, Jr.

Henry VIII Hotel and Conference
  Center, 124
  4690 North Lindbergh
  Bridgeton, MO 63044
  314/731-2777
  Mitch Julian

Nooter Corporation, 98-99
  1400 South Third Street
  St. Louis, MO 63104
  314/421-7211
  Robert H. Harper

Pet Incorporated, 104-105
  400 South Fourth Street
  St. Louis, MO 63102
  314/622-6114
  Thomas R. Pellett

St. Louis Post-Dispatch, 110-111
  900 North Tucker Boulevard
  St. Louis, MO 63101
  314/622-7236
  Dan Cotter

St. Luke's Hospital, 128-129
  232 South Woods Mill Road
  Chesterfield, MO 63107
  314/434-1500
  Patricia A. Treacy

Slay Industries, 106-107
  2001 South Seventh
  St. Louis, MO 63104
  314/772-7200
  Keith A. Rhodes

Sunnen Products Co., 100-103
  7910 Manchester Avenue
  St. Louis, MO 63143
  314/781-2100
  James K. Berthold

Thompson & Mitchell, 118-119
  One Mercantile Center
  St. Louis, MO 63101
  314/231-7676
  William G. Guerri

Index